Row Houses

This book is also available in a German language edition.
(ISBN 978-3-7643-7837-0)

Library of Congress Control Number: 2007932930

Translation from German into English
Usch Engelmann, Seattle

Graphic Design and Drawings: Sebastian Schaal, Martin Trefon
Assistance: Simon Gallner, Leon Schmidt

Bibliographic information published by the German National Library
The German National Library lists this publication in the Deutsche Nationalbibliografie; detailed bibliographic data are available on the Internet at http://dnb.d-nb.de.

Basel · Boston · Berlin
P.O. Box 133, CH-4010 Basel, Switzerland
Part of Springer Science+Business Media

Printed on acid-free paper produced from chlorine-free pulp. TCF ∞

Printed in Germany

ISBN: 978-3-7643-7838-7

9 8 7 6 5 4 3 2 1 www.birkhauser.ch

Günter Pfeifer and Per Brauneck

Row Houses

A Housing Typology

Birkhäuser
Basel · Boston · Berlin

Contents

Preface

Today, appreciating the ever-recurring as a quality seems like an anachronism. The term recurring or repetition has a negative connotation; it has become a synonym for monotony, sameness and boredom.

But the principle of repetition is always present and forms the basis of all life on our planet: pulse beat, breathing, the cycle of the seasons, to name just a few examples. The principle of repetition therefore also stands for continuity, reliability, stability and homogeneity – attributes that definitely carry positive denotation.

Repetition is a principle inherent to any structure. When we think of music, the importance of repetition to reveal coherence becomes apparent. First of all, there are rhythm and melody, both of which carry the composition. Varying tempi and variations of the melody lend the piece different colouration. One recognisable theme is repeated throughout the piece by carrying it through the composition and processing it. Only the repetition makes the composition understandable.

Luigi Snozzi, an architect from Ticino, once said: "If you have one good element, repeat it! ", and his work gives numerous examples for his virtuosic handling of the principle of repetition. Other architects besides him have also recognised and employed the potential of repetition.

The typology of row houses is based on this principle of repetition in the best sense – provided that the recurring element is worth repeating, and also provided that the method of repetition is not monotonous.

Our changing multifaceted living patterns do not allow monotony. Changing durations and habits of usage require new and flexible typologies. In addition, our socialisation patterns have increased and the cycles of individual reorientation have become shorter. Complex family and partnership structures have evolved which cannot be accommodated by traditional row house patterns.

These changes in today's living patterns constitute the motive for this series of books, which originated out of research conducted at the Department of Architecture at the University of Darmstadt. As part of this research work, one of the issues that has been addressed for some time now was that of a prospective typology training within the scope of designing residential buildings. Together with our students, we want to develop new building types that take current as well as future developments into consideration.

The series of books about residential building typology is not intended for students and architects alone, but also for "users" of architecture such as clients, building societies and developers. It shall inspire and, at best, lead to adapt known residential building patters to the requirements of today. Nothing is more persistent than habit; however, habit in most cases does not reflect current demands.

The first two volumes of this typology series are "Courtyard houses" and "Row houses", which systematically illustrate these two basic typologies with corresponding variants. These two simple basic types have in common that individual houses can be joined on two or three sides, thereby creating dense developments suitable for sustainable urban housing structures. The variety of house types is sorted by different categories in which the complexity of the types presented – originating partly from research projects and partly from built examples – increases in the course of the book. The illustrations are largely limited to floor plans, with complementary sectional drawings where needed. We abstained from including elevation drawings because in most cases they are not typologically relevant. The project descriptions call attention to particularities and point out possible difficulties (e.g. change of orientation). The built examples are illustrated similarly; the photographs chosen were selected to give an impression of the appearance of the house type presented. Information regarding construction and economics is largely not included; however, we do point out ecological advantages.

Holocaust Memorial, Berlin, Peter Eisenman

Cybernetics: Integration of type and topos

Today more than ever, residential architecture is bound to a multitude of value systems within a complex network of interdependencies. Therefore, typology can never be examined isolated from other factors. Rather, typological examinations form a platform displaying the many interdependencies that need to be considered. A systematic catalogue of building typologies such as this book might be of help for the designer. However, providing a practice-oriented mind with an architectural recipe book is very risky. On this note, it is necessary to integrate typology into the overall complex of contemporary creative thinking, in order to encourage an awareness of one's own doings.

The events and processes on our planet are extremely complex. At the threshold to the third millennium we are confronted with demanding challenges. Environmental changes, resource shortages, new economic phenomena and an ever-increasing world population are only a few of today's and future hot topics. In the face of these challenges, scientists demand that progress should not only be pushed on a technocratic and materialistic level, but that we also pioneer our structures of thinking and acting. The limitations of the classic methods of perception, based on the principle of dissection, become apparent. Expertise and atomisation of knowledge in ever smaller and specialised sub-areas alone will not be viable in the future.

The zeitgeist of timidity has taken hold of us all – of architects even more than of others. Enviously, we look at Buckminster Fuller, who left us gawping at his visions for living spaces in the Dymaxion House in the 1950s. An architect, who, 50 years ago, already gave us a telling-off about the influence of nature as a continuously systematic effect due to economic principles! For most of us he was a hopeless oddball. His patented geodetic cupola burnt down during the World Fair 1967 in Montreal: a signal heralding a long time without visionaries.

At the beginning of the 1960s, a few British architects founded the group Archigram, wanting us to believe that we could better live in bubble-shaped, air-conditioned flats with wall-integrated information systems than with Chippendale imitations. In Japan, visionaries also awoke around that time. Kenzo Tange created his design for the Tokyo Bay, Kurokawa designed cities lost in and resurged from the ocean. They called themselves metabolists, borrowed from the Greek word for change and vicissitude, based on the thoughts of Zen Buddhism.

Dymaxion house, Richard Buckminster Fuller

In Germany, Frei Otto – his first name meaning "free" and seemingly no coincidence – experimented with soap suds and bellows to detect the secret of the structures of thin bubbles. In 1964, he founded the Institute for Lightweight Plane Load-bearing Structures (IL) at the Technical University at Stuttgart, whose prototype became the model for the German pavilion at the World Fair in Montreal. All these people researching and designing on an experimental level were bound by the idea of creating new life styles and forms of society as well as by an irrepressible confidence in the future. America was competing for the moon; outer space was everywhere, in home movies, residential design and in the children's' rooms. What was this strange syndrome that afflicted us 50 years ago, and that no longer exists?

At the turn of the millennium our hopes still soared; giant domes, space labs and science centres were to paint our future. Computer-generated design bends lines, planes, spaces, distorts walls, and shreds rooftops. However, the new promises increasingly seem like formative self-admiration and a loquacious addiction to shape. A new millennium website on the Internet is filled with the most diverse contributions by politicians, authors, philosophers, sociologists, artists of all kind; architects, however, are mostly not represented.

Architecture has difficulties developing fundamentally new definitions. The established self-conception of the architect as a generalist can no longer be maintained when more and more detailed knowledge is required. Other disciplines have reacted to this situation by starting to rethink their approach. The goal is to think within a diverse network or use a system-oriented approach. This is the basis for cybernetics, which is applied in many scientific areas. The architect – in the traditional definition a mediator between different disciplines – already plans in a more or less networked environment. However, the term cybernetics has not yet been introduced to the field of architecture even though this particular strategy comprises many opportunities to develop sustainable architectural concepts.

The individual organisation of living spaces was unproblematic in the context described here as long as no more resources were used up than could grow again. The industrial revolution and subsequent decades, however, have led to a fundamental change of our way of living. The impact on the environment has increased dramatically and the human being has become the primary factor influencing the climate. Since 1950, the world energy requirement has almost quintupled. Currently, we use up as much fossil energy per year as nature produced over 500,000 years in the form of coal, crude oil and natural gas. At the beginning of the 21st century, saving energy and reducing CO_2 emissions are the most critical tasks, not only for architecture.

Building societies, developers and the clique of the real estate industry are often conspiring ignoramuses, who hide behind the so-called doable and the alleged desires of the user. The results are evident everywhere: in endless urban expansions and on the boundaries of grown villages. As dignified houses and our memories rot away in the village centres, detached houses in new residential developments in the shape of prefabricated houses called Chalet, Lifestyle, Ambience, Future, Residence or Metropolitan are booming. Unfulfilled longings and desires, identified by these names, in this context remain without perspectives; future demands or changes are not considered or, if modifications of size or combinations with other units are possible, these are designed for growth, not for downsizing. Behind all this, paradoxically and abruptly, lies an undefined and nebulous quest for authenticity even though nobody really knows what this exactly means. Germany's population, for example, has long since reached a level at which we can question the entire system of detached and row houses. The share of singles has risen to 36%, the number of couples with two children stagnates at 7.7% (source: Federal Statistical Office 2003). Who then will live in these flats, specifically designed for small families?

At the same time, the dynamics within medical science, genetic engineering, neurology, and information technology are breathtaking. Life can be prolonged more and more. The pharmaceutical industry promises longer life spans, youth, potency, and eroticism at any age. We have to fear that the application of genetic engineering is determined by our new global religion – which for some time has been known as science. The psychosocial, cultural and social effects are unforeseeable. And we wonder why there are no visions for future living! Torpor would be too limited a term to describe the dynamics in the area of residential living.

To architecturally cope with the task of residential living, we need a change of perception that leaves behind our linear mechanistic view of the world, coined by western culture, and embraces a circulation model based on communication and integration. The cybernetic principle can support a paradigm shift in this direction within architectural theory – a theory that no longer works off current practices in a backward-oriented fashion, but prospectively, forward-looking, opens up new perspectives. The principles of cybernetics shall lead to a new perception that will influence the structure and appearance of architecture. Such a change in perspective will have an impact on methodological approaches and prerequisites of design as well as on the definition of goals for future-oriented building.

Building means nothing more than to interfere with an ecological, sensitively balanced system, with the objective of the creation of a new balance and extensive self-regulation of the installed systems later on. Not only the data of the immediate surroundings should be included in the concept; rather, an encompassing analysis of the different interferences with the global ecological balance is necessary. Cybernetic building methods are based on a networked system of functional elements that interact with each other. The goal is to integrate all elements – including structural, passive and active elements such as the use of daylight, sun protection, artificial light, glare protection, activated building components, controlled ventilation as well as the use of rainwater and wind – into an all-encompassing overall concept.

From this perspective, visions can no longer be limited to being of technical nature. In only a few years, it will be possible to develop buildings that can create a balance with nature. And the amount of technology necessary to achieve this goal will ultimately be irrelevant. New materials can store and insulate, are translucent and strong, and offer more structural stability than all materials we have ever used in construction. In a broader perspective, hydrogen and electrolysis will make us independent of today's energy suppliers;

cars will be exhaust-free, running on hydrogen, and the remaining crude oil will be processed into precious plastic products. Communication technology will globally network every participant with everything. This is the main difference compared to the visions of the 1960s. Then, in the 1970s, there was an unshakeable belief in technology. We believed that we could only control technology if we kept everything separate. In the cities, we separated pedestrian traffic from car traffic on different levels – even encompassing buildings – and in overpasses and underpasses. We separated living space from workspace, we invented centres for administration and banking, we separated old people from young people, etc. Today, we know better.

Current visions are different. Architecture can provide us also with dreams of movement. It is the movement of changed life styles and savoir vivre that cannot be described by floating architecture with slants and curves. In a time of de-separation of individual and collective living patterns, our familiar images have lost their validity. Society offers multi-optional patterns everywhere. A multifaceted division of different psychological worlds, the complexity of different and changing living conditions that last ever shorter and therefore become more fragmented (work and partnerships), lead to numerous experiential relations. A "multiphrenic" situation has evolved, which is so present today that we experience it as an everyday phenomenon.

Group of houses "De Landtong", Rotterdam, Frits van Dongen

We have to comprehend our living spaces in the same multifaceted way. One of the fundamental insights must be that a building not only uses up but also generates energy. This does not only relate to the thermal comfort, but also to the individual bodily sculpture and the satisfaction of psychological and social parameters such as feeling comfortable and at home.

Residential structures today hardly accommodate these factors at all. If we want to transfer the social situation to dwellings, we need to consider certain transformations of "movement". We need to combine nomadism and settledness, as well as the individuality of a private urban retreat and lively interactive alliances. Instead of segregation of any kind, integration on all levels is the main criterion for current visions. After a millennium of specialisation and inventions but also segregation, the new millennium is all about integration.

Building structures of the future will be able to offer this kind of interconnectedness. Living spaces will form a spatial network arranged in small and large units of different density. Figures (positive volumes) create grounds (negative volumes) which can serve as open or interactive spaces. Differentiated building levels and volumes create spaces of varying privacy and publicness; some can be utilised at the user's discretion, some are fixed. This system allows enclosed flats as well as an open weave of spaces for interactions and private spaces of different size and zoning density. The size of the overall building structure is designed to accommodate changing group sizes with different needs and orientations – socially, culturally, and sociologically. The system offers work and exchange of services as well as options for participatory organised sections within the housing development.

Today's building technology can fulfil all these requirements. What is missing is an integrated social and architectural model that is no longer based on segregation. Future ways of living will have to return to relying more on self-organisation of communities and groups. Work will be part of life up to old age because its definition has changed. Patchwork families will become multi-generation patchwork families of varying productivity and activity within a network of affinities and multi-relationships.

Architectural reality clearly lags behind our sociological reality. This is not only caused by the architects' capability to persist alone, as he or she deals much more with shapes than with context. The awareness that a stronger consideration of the overall energy budget of a building is necessary has fortunately increased in the minds of planners, users and manufacturers. However, the process is still mostly uncoordinated; individual measures are simply added to each other and they only relate to the physical energy budget of a building. When, today, we talk about ecologic construction, we think of sun collectors on the roof, thick thermal insulation packages, maybe of a cistern for grey water use. In the end, all these measures are saddled onto the existing image of a house rather than integrating it typologically. The method is not only ineffective from an energetic standpoint, since this additive approach does not produce any synergy effects.

As little as one century ago, the pragmatic strategy of a more or less direct translation of contextual conditions and necessities led to authentic house types; authentic, here, meaning that interior structure, way of living and user habits as well as the exterior shape have melted into one entity. Today, we bemoan the lack of authentic structures. Technical and mechanical innovations have allowed us to largely ignore all contextual conditions. If the image of a corporation or institution requires a high-rise building with a glass façade, this wish can be fulfilled. The question of how user-friendly and liveable a building is has been reduced to the question of how much performance the technical equipment can offer. The value of being able to recognise one's environment as well as the personal sensation of comfort has suffered from this "anything is possible" attitude. This is because the complex interaction of type and topos is part of our inherent knowledge. We intuitively sense the congruence of type and topos; reciprocally, we also sense the lack of this concordance. As a conclusion of the interrelations outlined herein, we can say that the cybernetic planning process aims at the integration of type and topos. The main issues that will lead to a continuous transformation of the house types are:

- social interaction and adaptation to individual sociological demands across all stages of life,
- the changing working conditions,
- the issues of energy, resources and ecological balance,
- the change of the topos considering embedding and adaptation to the historical and urban context,
- the individual perception of phenomenon such as atmosphere, light, materials and memories.

Façade of a residential house, Seoul

The principle of repetition

The row house type does not necessarily have an immediate positive connotation. Worker's cottages from the beginning of industrialisation served more to increase the profits of the enterprise than to fulfil the needs of the occupants – at least viewed from today's perspective. Stringing together absolutely identical units can lead to banal linear structures, lacking any kind of urban accentuation. The row apparently does not meet the desire for individuality nor does its arrangement create a comfortable degree of privacy.

The strength of the row house as a building type definitely lies in its economic advantages. The simple and rational principle of adding on makes it possible to erect a large number of dwellings within a short time frame. In addition, the capability of joining units with others leads to a well-balanced ratio of living space, surface area and volume, which in turn creates advantageous characteristics in terms of energy efficiency. And when circulation areas are designed intelligently, the row house type offers many possibilities to increase or decrease the size of the individual unit. Combinations are easier manageable than, for example, those of courtyard houses (see volume 1 of this series), which require managing connections in three directions.

Therefore, the row house type certainly has potential for further developments. Such developments need to solve the above mentioned typological weaknesses related to individuality and privacy. One of these challenges is to create open spaces without resorting to partition walls excessively used today. Terraces on the upper floors, for example, could remedy the problem. Also the entrance side needs special consideration when talking about individuality. In this context, individuality does not so much refer to design attributes, but rather the task of creating a sensitive transition from the public area to the entrances that are lined up like pearls on a string. A weather-protected secluded open space in front of the entrance door can be very important for the sensation of entering one's own house.

The configuration of the entrances controls the logic of the exterior orientation and access zones, which, at best, also structures the public space. This is a problem of the monotone row structure that needs to be resolved by developing appropriate corner or end houses. Variations within the row can produce directional changes and interruptions and a rhythm is created by modifying the basic house type.

The generally two-sided orientation leads to variations within the row related to its orientation. A south-facing row house can generate heat gains.

Living and recreational areas in that case all need to face south. As a result, secondary rooms as intermediate temperature zones as well as the entrance areas typically face north. Due to the orientation, the depth of the house is smaller than that of an east-west oriented row.

The width of the house basically depends on whether one or two personal rooms per floor are oriented towards one side. In the case of two rooms, the clear width between the party walls lies between at least 4.50 metres up to comfortable 7.30 metres. From a width of around 5.20 metres it is possible to arrange a straight stairway in a crosswise fashion. Thus, multiple variations can be realised compared to the single-axis type with a lengthwise staircase.

Several row houses, Amsterdam

The positioning and type of the staircase is of great significance when looking at the floor plan typology of a row house. A central position within the floor plan is important to provide minimal circulation areas on the upper storeys. Widened access spaces can serve to eliminate mono-functional access areas. Spaces that can manage a certain degree of publicity within the house would be the best choice: office and workspaces, kitchens or rooms with multi-functional uses. Split-level staircases with landings opening up towards adjoining rooms can also aid in eliminating mono-functional circulation areas and can simultaneously create a spatial continuum across several storeys.

Interior space of Kirchhölzle, Schopfheim, Günter Pfeifer

Functionally unspecified rooms will become increasingly important for modern floor plans since they provide the occupant with the highest degree of flexibility. In these rooms the position of doors and windows and the size of the room are particularly important. A room with between twelve and 16 square metres floor space offers numerous possibilities for different uses such as a personal room, office or living space, especially if wall openings are not located too close to the corners and therefore eliminate usable floor space. A different strategy could be to concentrate the increasing demand for more storage space in so-called service zones that can also accommodate utility cores. The principle of the "thick wall" comprising functional elements such as staircase, toilet, storage, bed, desk or built-in cupboards is a proven approach for furnishing flexible floor plans.

The personal room's importance within a flexible floor increases significantly. Dedicating specific rooms as master bedroom or children's room – as is still done in many floor plans – is no longer valid when considering today's changeable life partnerships and patchwork families. The personal room's character will become increasingly private. Also, individual intimate spaces such as shower and toilet gain in importance so that the span from public to private within a house will become larger over time.

The row house cannot be eliminated from the variety of residential house types due to its extreme cost effectiveness. The problems that designers are confronted with when planning row houses are solvable. However, they need to be addressed and can lead to creative solutions, as is documented by the examples given in this book. These solutions should nevertheless be understood as prototypical only, and for specific applications need to be cybernetically – in the sense outlined in this text – woven into their context.

Floor plan types

The different possibilities for arranging floor plans within the row house type are primarily determined by the circulation within the house. The position of the staircase is the factor that defines the different row house types. In combination with the position of the entrance and the proportion of the footprint of the house, it determines the specific of this house type. An energy-conscious arrangement of the floor plan generates additional house types.

Without staircase

The single-storey row house type is the simplest form of arrangement. The large depth of the floor plan requires recesses or cut-outs. Generously dimensioned inner courtyards provide sufficient daylight and create light-flooded floor plans.

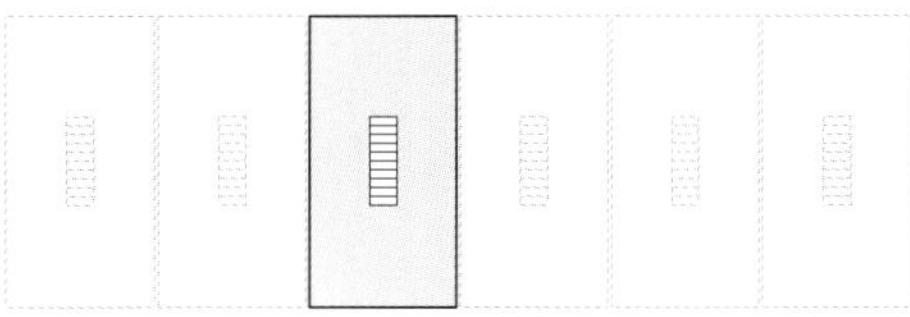

Longitudinal staircase

Since the floor plan of the row house type is usually deeper than wide, this is the most common form of arrangement. Depending on the width of the house, the staircase is located either along the party wall or between room axes. The depth of the floor plan usually calls for an east-west orientation.

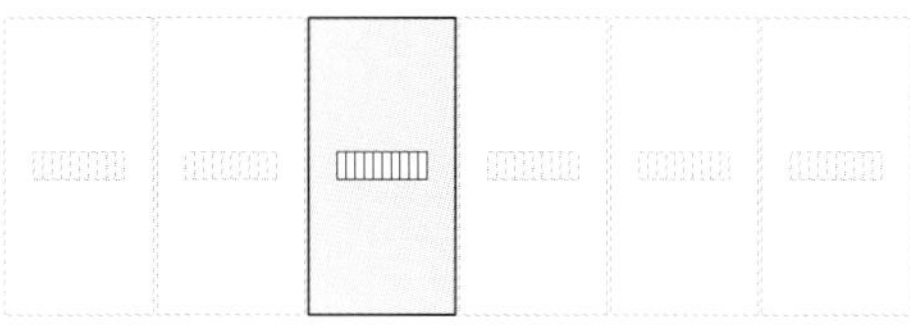

Transversal staircase

The transversal staircase requires a wider floor plan. Usually this type comprises at least two personal rooms on the side of the house that is exposed to daylight. This floor plan allows for small house depths and provides the option of a single-sided orientation towards the south.

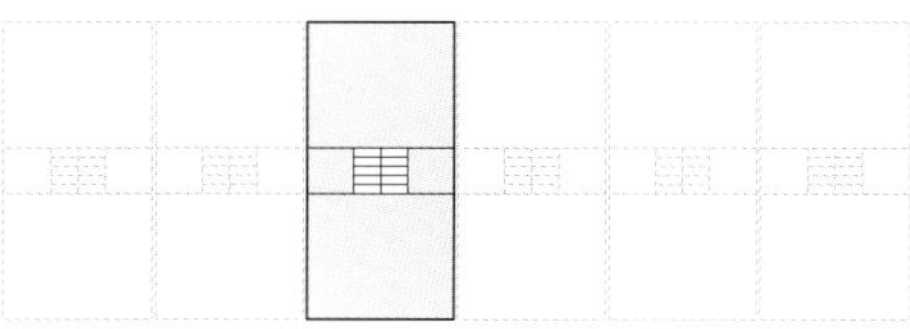

Longitudinal split-level

Shifts of levels in the longitudinal direction of the house creates a dynamic spatial atmosphere. The position of the staircase defines the proportions of the individual levels. Voids between the offsets create visual connections and offer daylight options for the centre sections of the floor plan.

Transversal split-level

In the house type with transversal split levels, each half-storey level can recei-ve daylight from two sides. The offset across the long side of the floor plan creates numerous spatial design and daylight options.

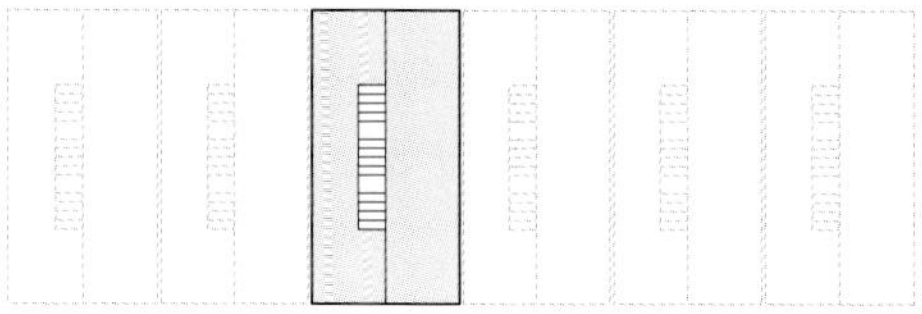

Back-to-back

This house type is the prototype of spatial efficiency and is ideally suited for dense housing development structures. Due to its one-sided orientation towards the access side, the possibilities of this type initially seem limited. Only in combination with patios or roof terraces does it shows it full potential.

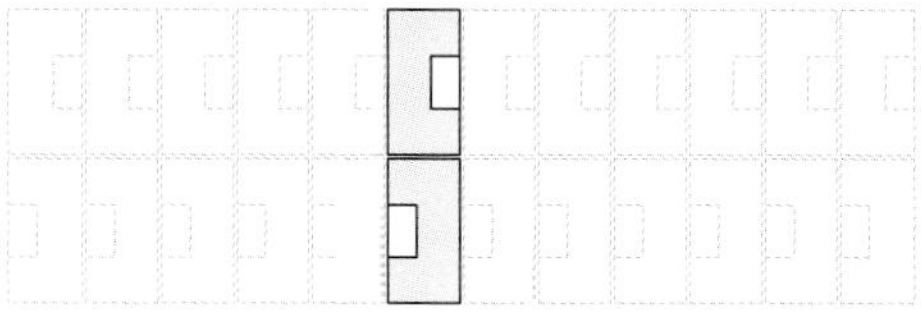

Front-to-back

This house type overcomes the deficit of a one-sided orientation with an intelligently arranged circulation. The floor plans of the apartment units shift from one side of the house to the other on each floor. Due to this interlocked arrangement, each unit receives daylight from the west and east.

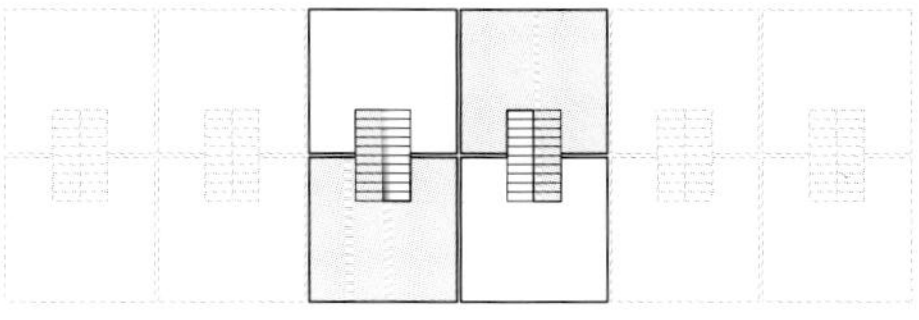

Back-to-back, "vis-à-vis"

This version of the back-to-back house type is connected only on the lower levels. On the upper levels, tower-like extensions with central access allow daylight from all sides and orientation in any direction. The roof area above the ground floor can be used as secluded open spaces.

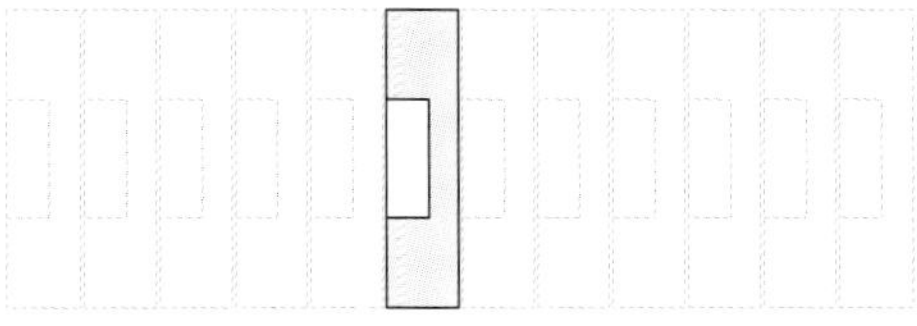

Two-zone house

In addition to circulation being the main criterion for the arrangement of the floor plan, the idea of an energetically efficient floor plan leads to an expansion of the typology. New house types evolve by creating zones with different room temperatures within the house.

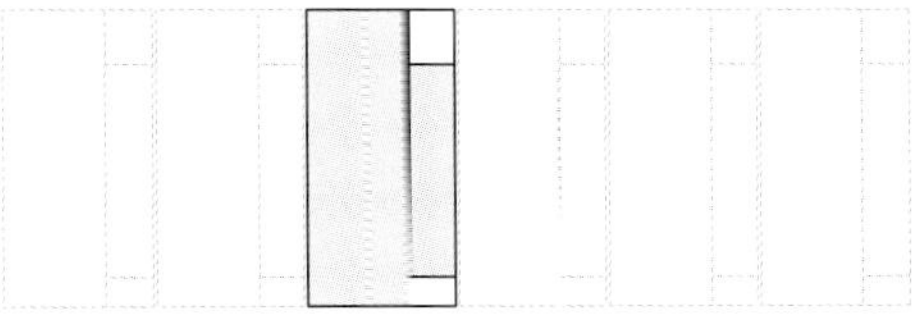

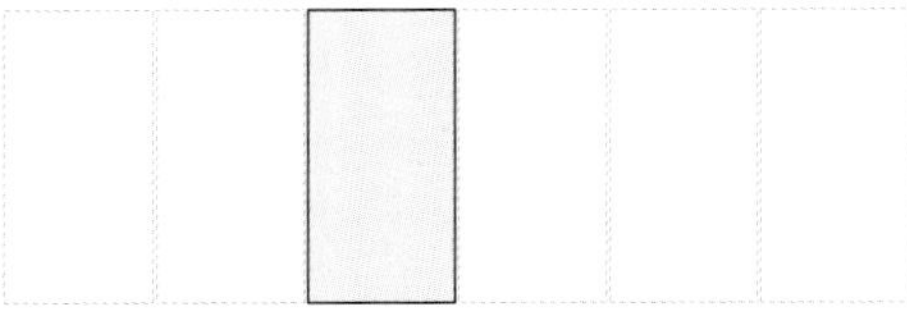

Without staircase
Single storey
North-south orientation

This large-area row house with an integrated garage is well structured. The living and dining room faces south and receives natural light via the courtyard, which also serves as an entry yard. The small entryway, an economical distribution space, is lit from above and provides easy access to the rather small rooms. Dimensions in plan as well as ceiling heights can be modified. The north-south orientation can be changed to an east-west orientation if the courtyard faces west. The structure of the residential development should be based on the assumption that no further areas of the property will be occupied other than by the house and setbacks to the north and south. Thus implemented, this structure is an economical house type, not least because of its simple construction. To access the house via the closed-in courtyard can be disadvantageous as the intimate character of the courtyard is impaired by this function.

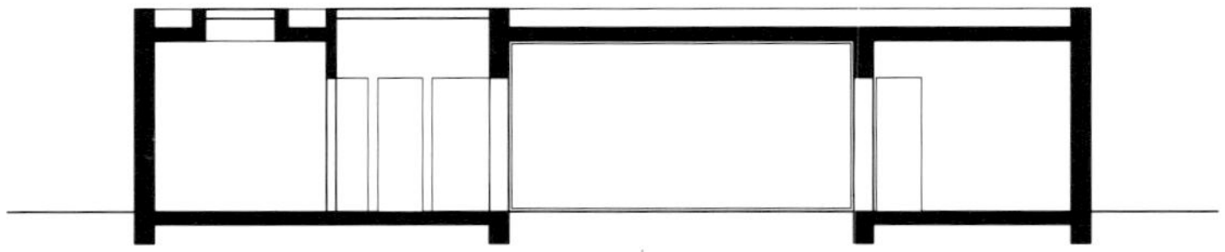

Longitudinal section

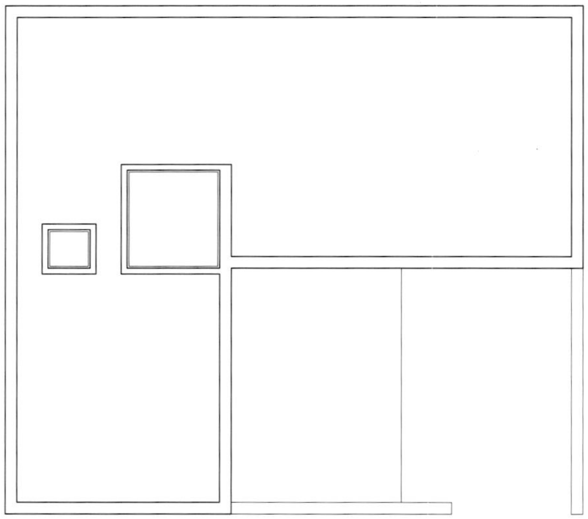

Top view of the roof

Group of houses
Berlin, 1999
Roland Schweitzer

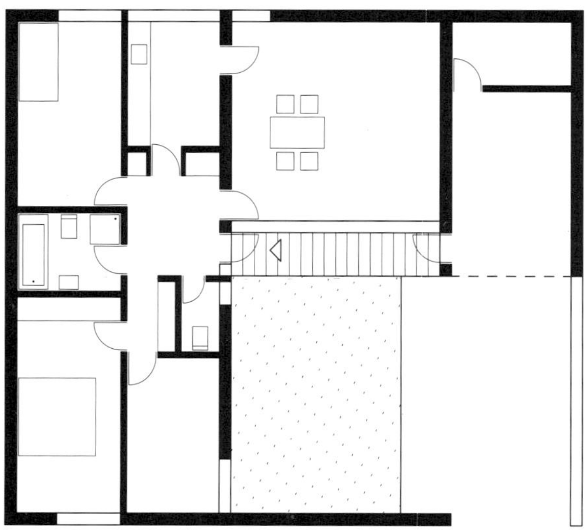

Ground floor

Without staircase
Single storey
North-south orientation

This house type, with 36 metres unusually deep, clearly depicts the characteristics and issues of single-storey row houses. Due to the narrow width of the house, sufficient daylight illumination can only be accomplished by organising the personal rooms around an inner courtyard. The interior and exterior spaces are tightly interlocked by indentations in the overall volume to create space for an entry yard with service rooms and a parking space on the north side, and for a protected open space providing daylight for an additional room on the south side. This house type functions with hardly any hallways. The elongated north-south alignment can be differentiated into several functional zones – open kitchen, dining, working, and living area. Depending on the specific property dimensions, the width and depth of the house can be optimised. Different ceiling heights or staggered levels are also possible, which enables this type to accommodate different topographic conditions.

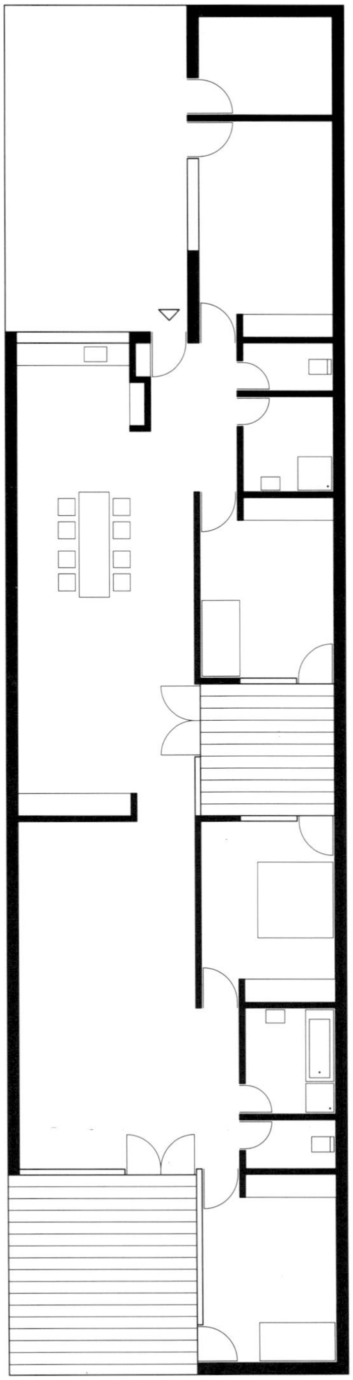

Ground floor

Top view of the roof

Student project
Darmstadt University
Katja Fischer

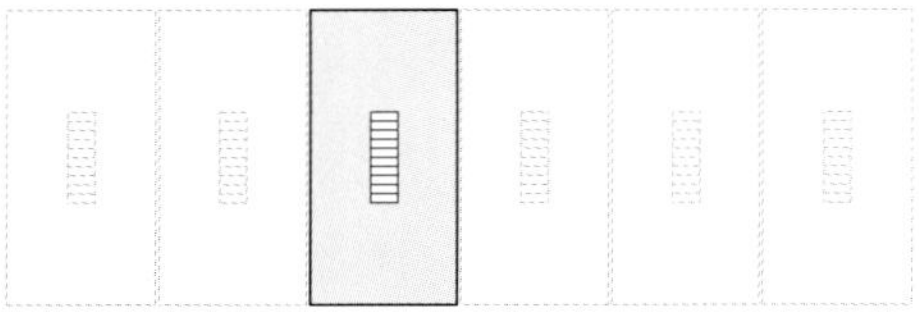

Longitudinal staircase
Two storeys
East-west orientation

The access to the first floor with a single-flight staircase arranged on the side of the house allows for a spacious, open living area with dining space and kitchen on the ground floor. The kitchen is integrated in a built-in cupboard running the whole length of the house. A simple hatch in the floor of the small porch serves as access to the partial basement. The first floor comprises two personal rooms facing east and west respectively. The bathroom is opposite to the staircase, between the personal rooms. The staircase area is sky-lit. The inner bathroom could also receive natural light by installing a skylight. A balcony in front of the larger personal room on the first floor provides the necessary sun protection for the living room below. In principle, this house type can also be arranged with a north-south orientation. Its dimensions can be modified; a full basement is possible, as is a second floor.

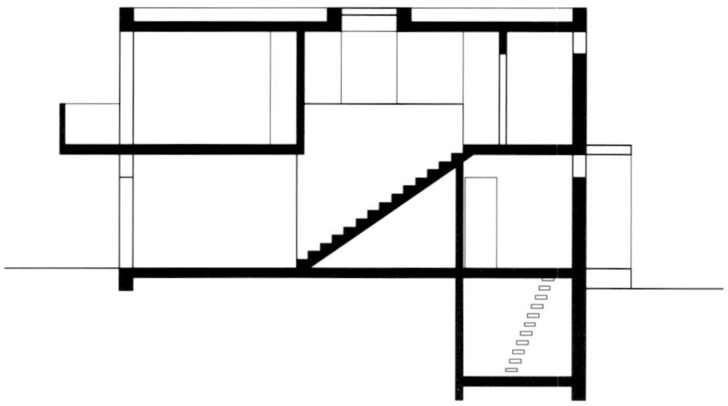

Longitudinal section

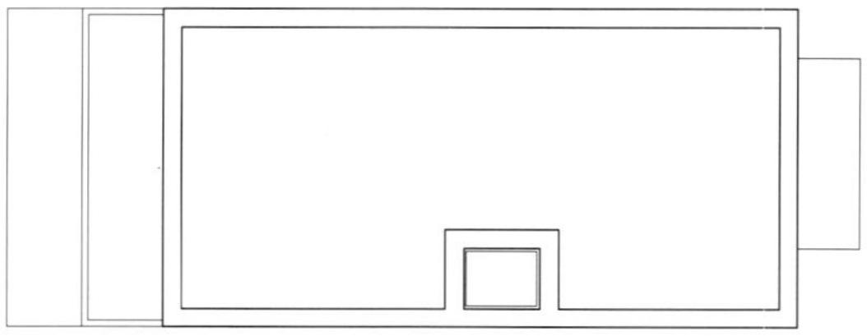

Top view of the roof

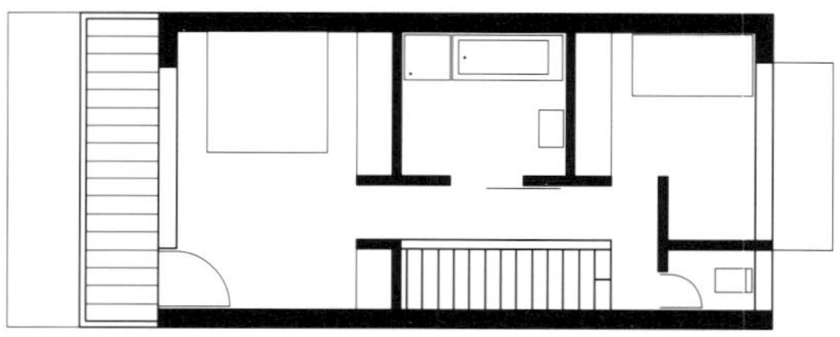

Upper floor

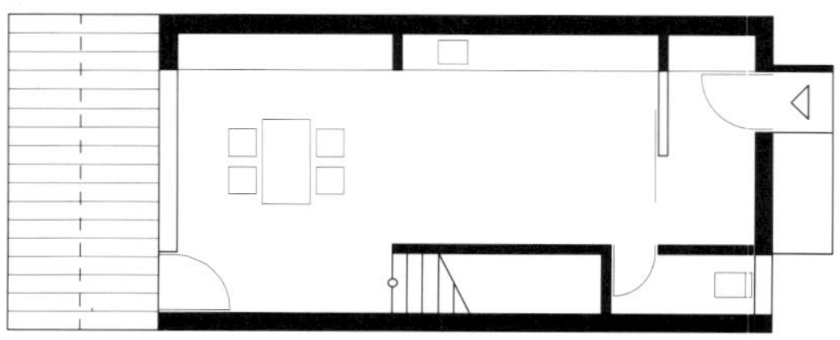

Ground floor

Group of houses "Falkenweg"
Dornbirn, 2002
Johannes Kaufmann

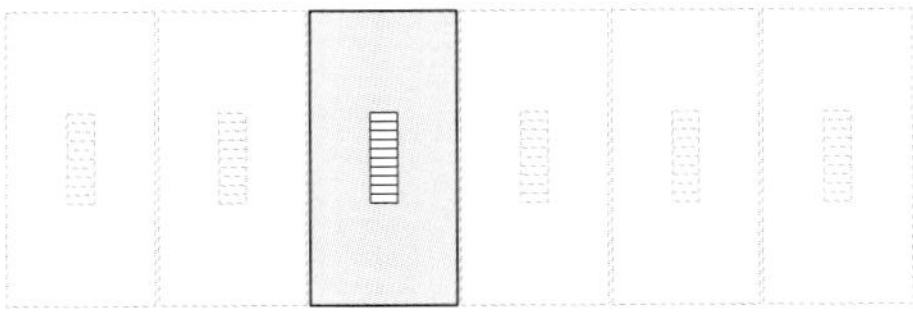

Longitudinal staircase
Two storeys
North-south orientation

This house type is characterised by its symmetric zoning and a two-storey atrium-type space in the middle of the floor plan. Economical access is provided via the landing of a double-flight staircase. The two-storey fully glazed "energy garden" on the south side offers passive solar heat gains. The adjoining rooms as well as the rooms facing south on the upper floor can profit from the light output and heat gain it provides. In addition to these advantages, the small house visually feels much bigger than it actually is and has a generous flair. The house type, shown here with an optimum economical layout, can be enlarged at the users' discretion. A steeper roof pitch could create a top floor providing further rooms. To maximise energy gain, this house type should be oriented towards the south. However, it can also be arranged in an east-west orientation.

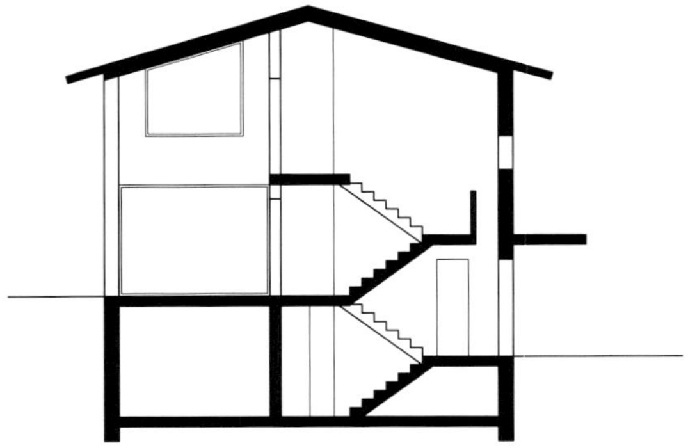

Cross section

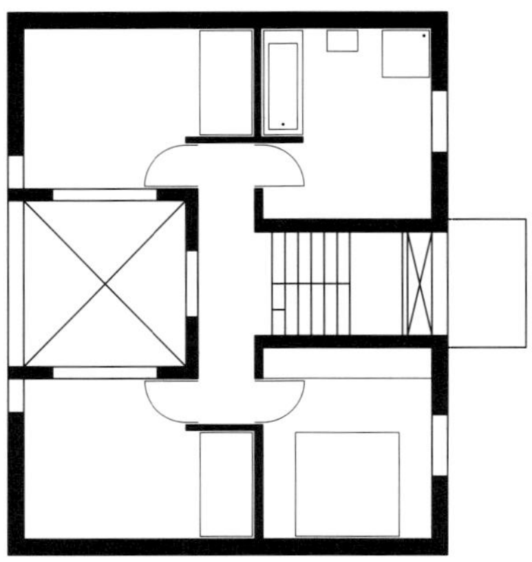

Upper floor

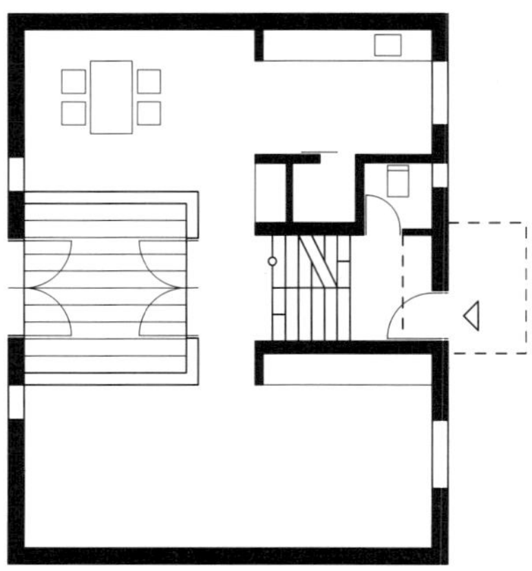

Ground floor

Solar houses
Donaueschingen, 1994
Harry Ludszuweit

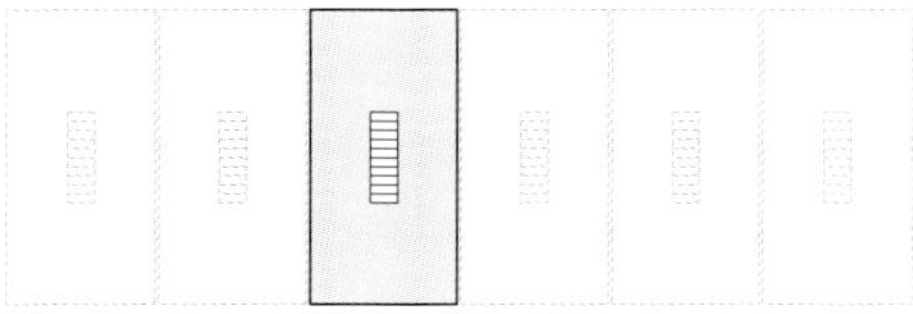

Longitudinal staircase
Two storeys
North-south orientation

The concept of this house type allows it to accommodate up to four flats of different sizes by simple modifications. The basic type comprises two attached houses, with two or three window axes each. The room in the centre axis between the staircases can be allocated to either one of the units. The rooms on the first floor are arranged at an offset to the partitioning on the ground floor – a small ground floor unit with a large first floor or vice versa.
As the staircase leads directly from the porch to the first floor, the two levels can be accessed individually.
Additional exterior space on the first floor can easily be created by adding a balcony above the ground level open space. This house type requires an east-west orientation. Instead of a basement, a zone with secondary rooms is allocated in front of the houses.

Group of houses "Sackpfeife"
Weimar, 1998
Walter Stamm-Teske

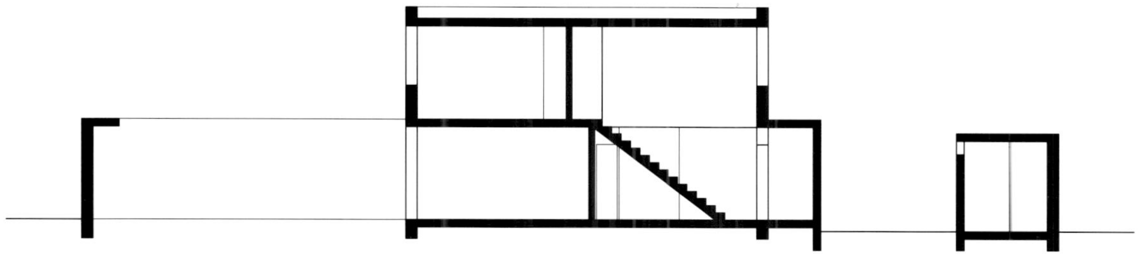

Longitudinal section

Upper floor

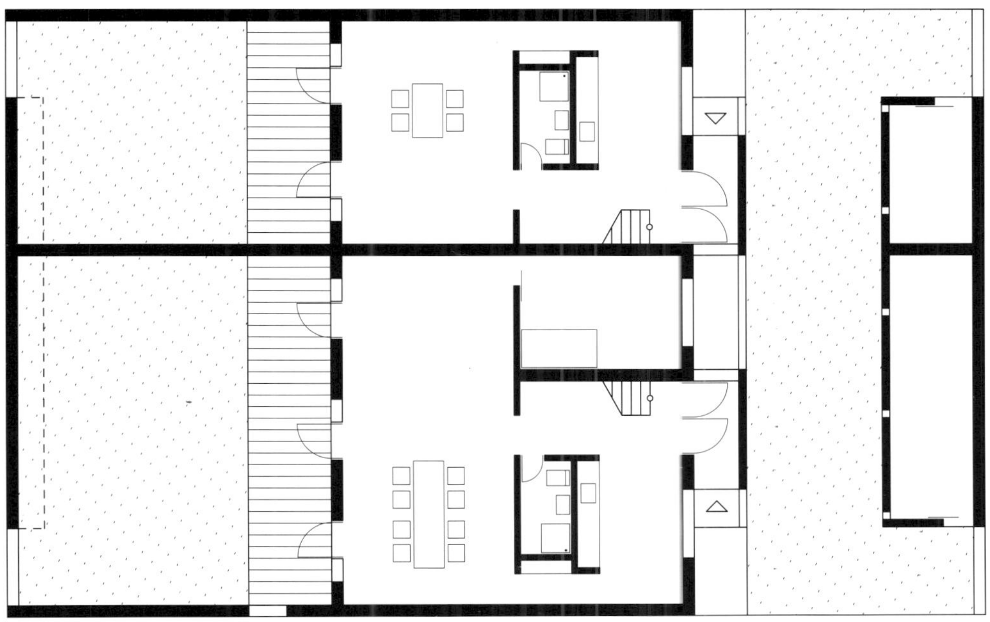

Ground floor

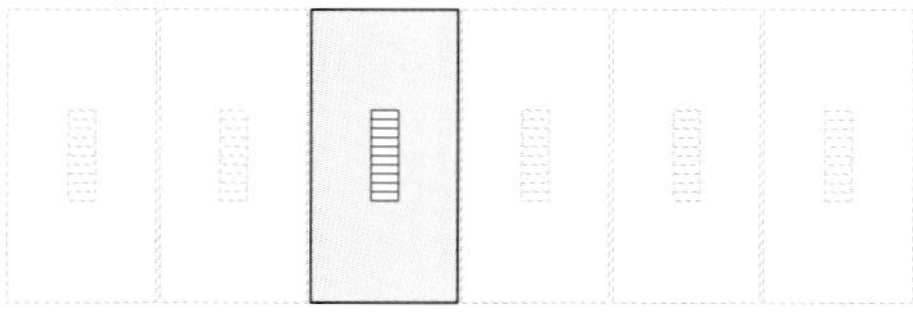

Longitudinal staircase
Two storeys
North-south orientation

This house type is defined by a parking space inside the building. The garage, located in the basement, is accessed via a ramp. Elevating the entrance level above site level shortens the length of the ramp. A form of exterior corridor leads to the entrance area. It is set six steps above site level and connects all houses with each other. The different heights are compensated in the living room, which is located six steps below the entry level. The dining area and kitchen are situated on the generously dimensioned mezzanine, which is the characteristic element of this house type due to the fully glazed kitchen wall and an additional door connecting to the exterior corridor. The first floor has three well-proportioned bedrooms. A small loggia is located in front of the north-facing children's room. Due to a cut-out in the building, a west-facing mono-pitch roof provides sufficient west light for the room below and the inner bathroom.

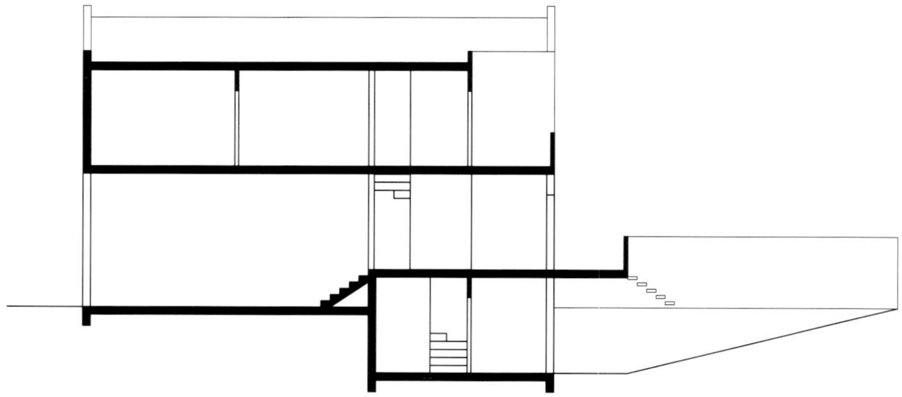

Longitudinal section

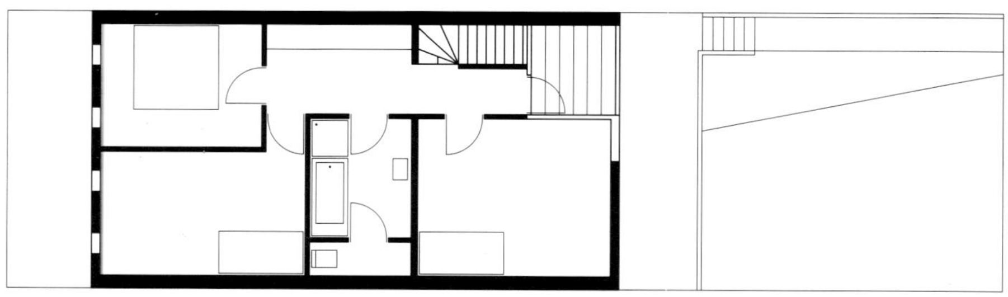

Upper floor

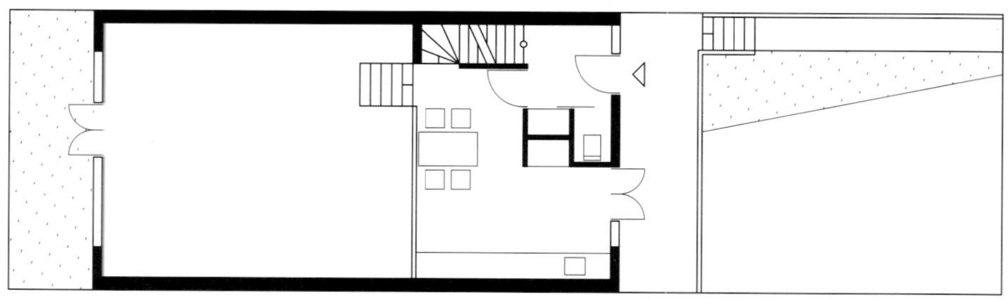

Ground floor

Thomas de Beer houses
Tilburg, 1996
Neutelings Riedijk

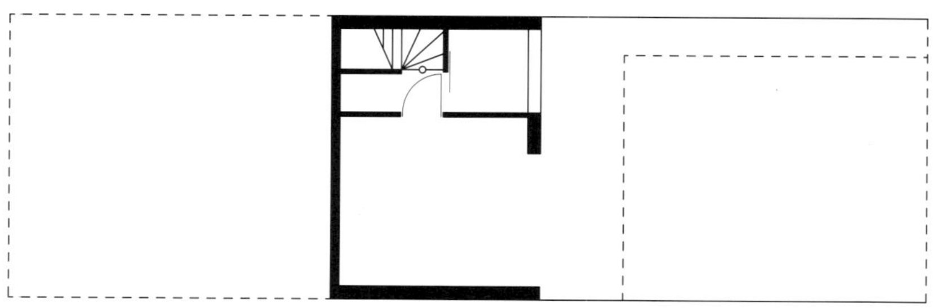

Basement

19
18

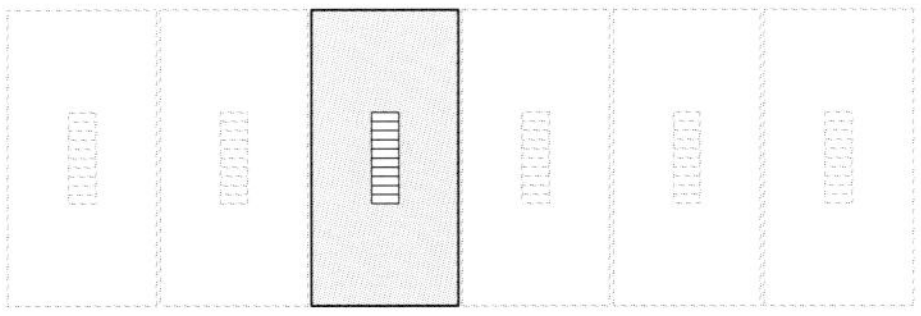

Longitudinal staircase
Two storeys
North-south orientation

This house type is zoned such that all living areas and bedrooms face south. The entrance to the house and secondary rooms are located on the north side. The open staircase as an integral part of the living space is arranged in such a way that it creates a generous distribution zone on the first floor providing space to play and work. The location of the staircase in the centre of the building allows this house type to be configured with different dimensions. The basic types are houses with four or six rooms. Secondary uses on the ground floor (laundry room, playroom, etc.) lead to units with five to seven rooms. Separate garden houses on the ground level accommodate additional secondary rooms. This arrangement creates small intimate open spaces. Adding a basement is possible; however, this would eliminate the open staircase in the living area. Due to the timber construction, the span of this house type is small. The dimensions of the basic type can easily be modified.

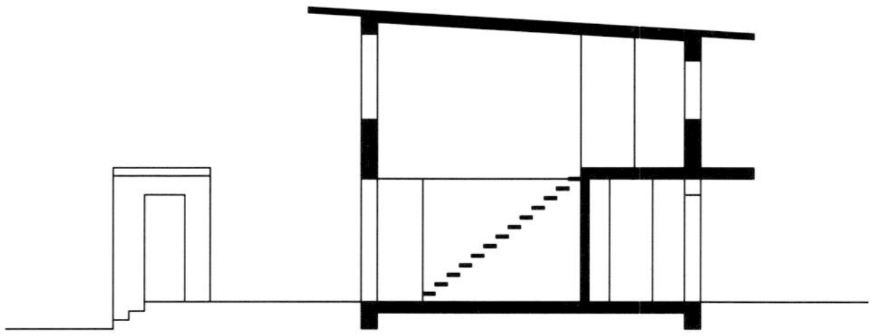

Cross section

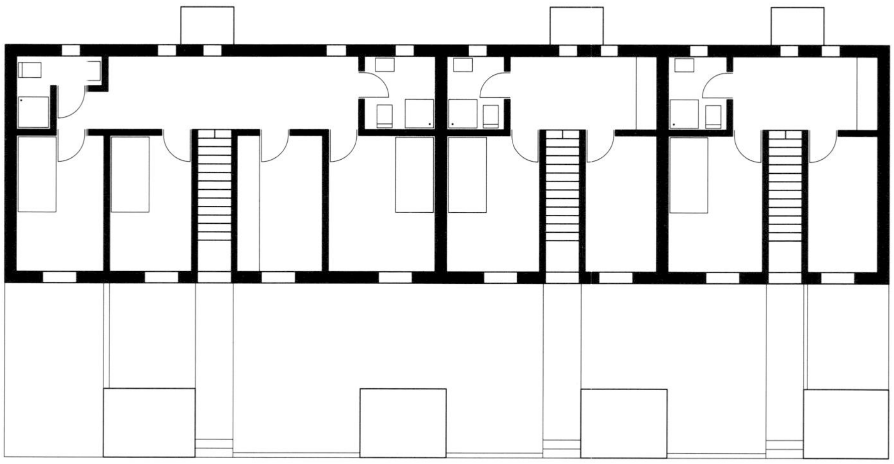

Upper floor

Ecumenical residential house
Darmstadt, 1998
Günter Pfeifer

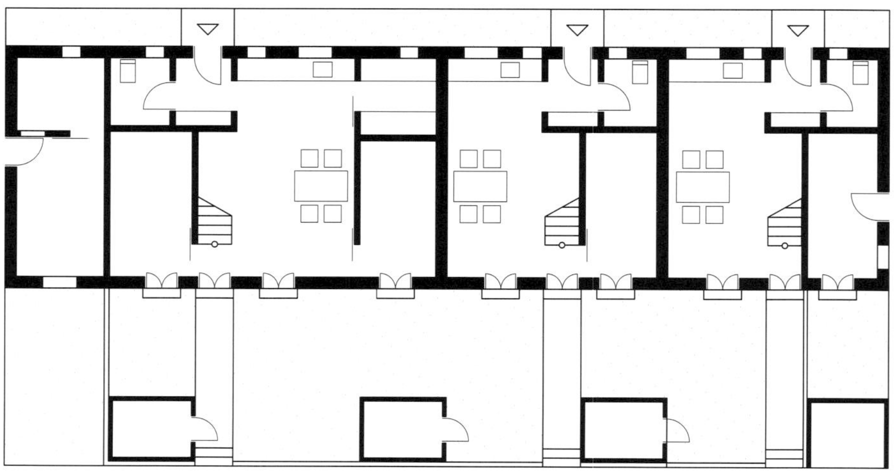

Ground floor

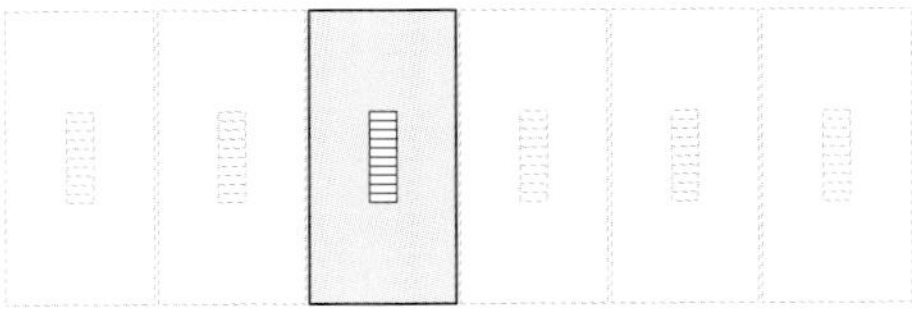

Longitudinal staircase
Two storeys
East-west orientation

This narrow row house with its landing staircase in the longitudinal direction of the house allows for flexible subdivision into different apartment units. Personal rooms are located in the half-basement and on the first floor. The living and dining area is to be found on the middle floor level, which is slightly raised. Each personal room can be accessed independently of the central living area via the staircase located directly at the entrance. Thus, all rooms can be inhabited independently of each other. The location of the staircase on the side of the structure enables a linking with parts of the adjoining row house. Located half a storey above the entrance level, the living area with a two-storey open space opens towards the garden without allowing views from the exterior into the house. The deeply recessed façade on the garden side creates a protected open space. A parking area is located on the entrance side in the half-basement. It can also be used as a personal room. A weak point of this house type are the bathrooms that receive no daylight.

Group of houses "Serrewoningen"
Tilburg, 1998
Bedaux de Brouwer

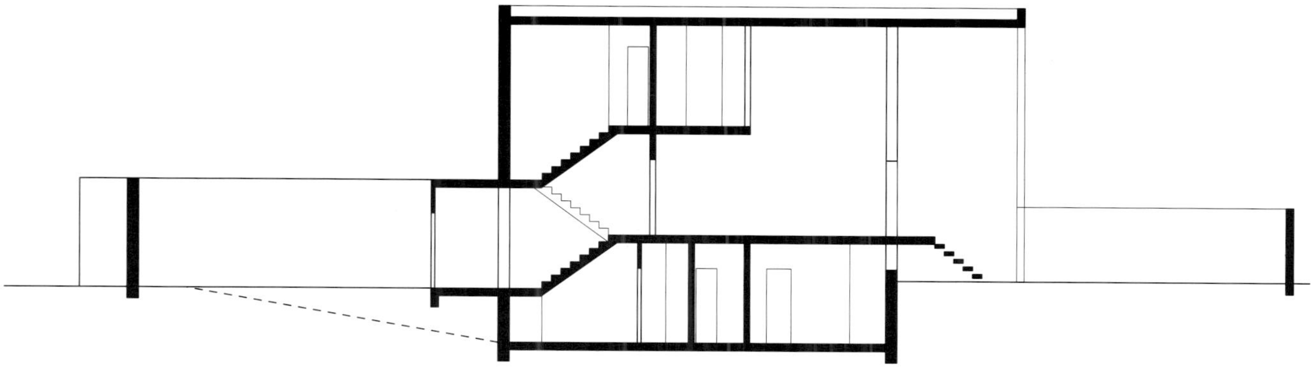

Longitudinal section

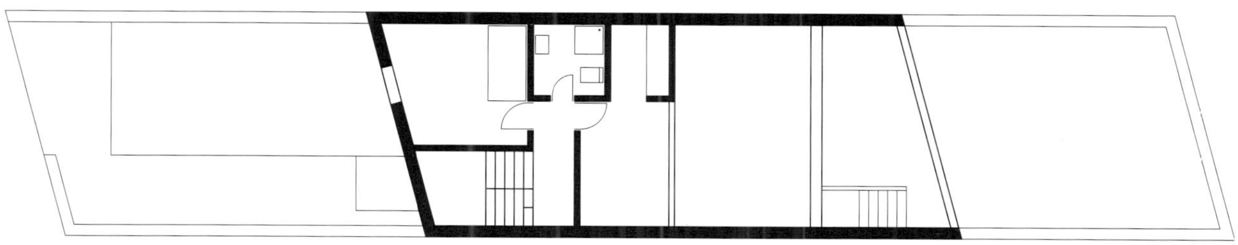

Top floor

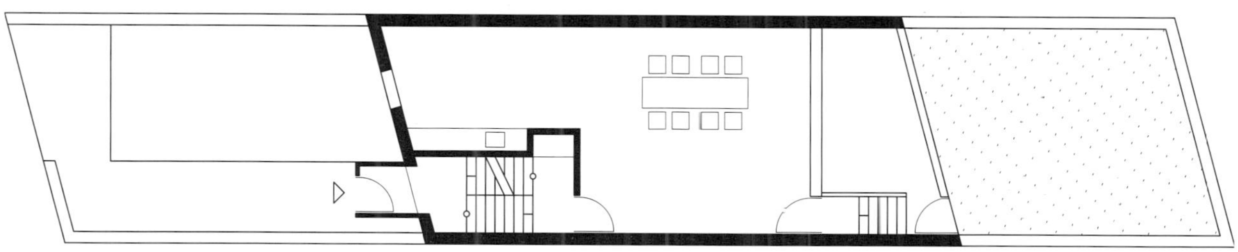

Ground floor

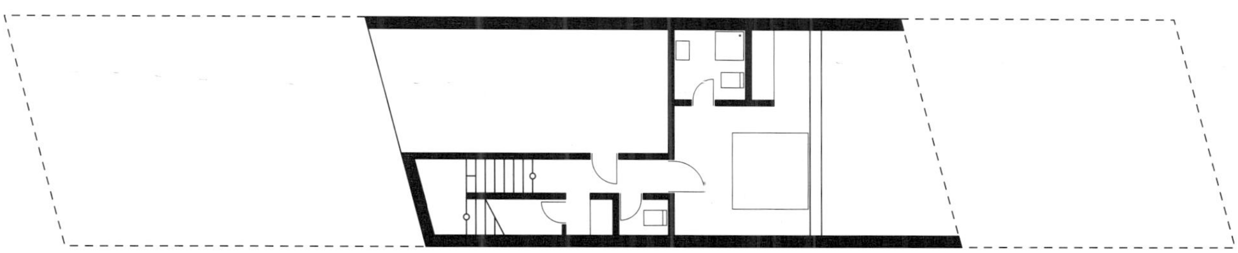

Basement

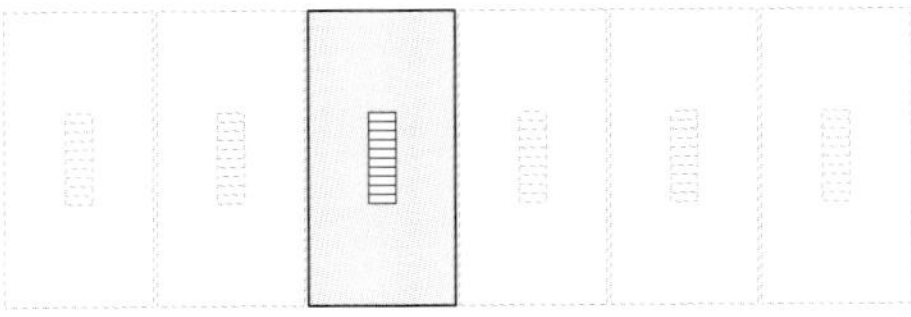

Longitudinal staircase
Three storeys
East-west orientation

Two or three storeys – one might wonder when looking at this house. Its basement is in no way a regular basement as it extends too far above the ground. While the house is accessed on the east side on the lowest level, the actual living space is located on the ground floor. The staircase leading outside also serves as a seating area and a piece of "action furniture". The basement is therefore activated to serve additional living purposes – as a room for hobbies or a play area complementing the children's rooms, which are mostly very small, on the upper floors. The layout of the upper floors is very restricted. However, considering that this house comprises three personal rooms, a living and dining area with kitchen as well as a large multi-purpose room, its economical use of space is impressive. The construction of this house type is as simple as it is economical; it even lends itself to self-construction and can be executed with various materials. A connection with adjoining units could be realised via the basement.

Residential area "Pilotengasse"
Vienna, 1992
Herzog & de Meuron

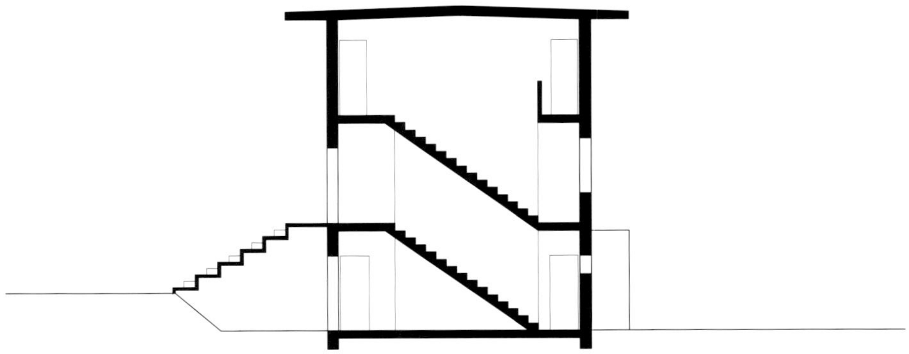

Cross section

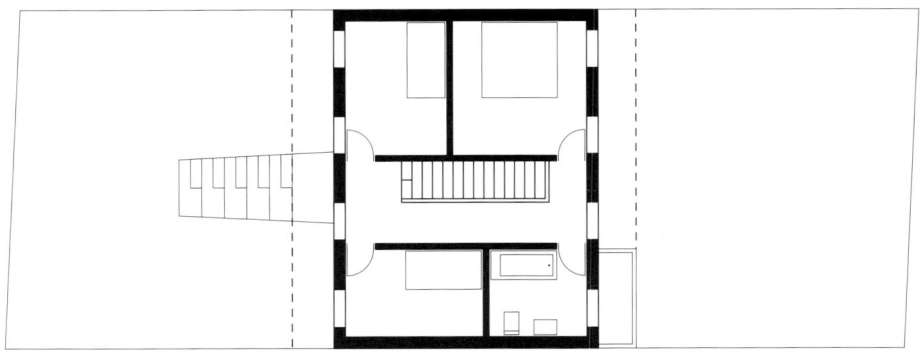

2nd upper floor

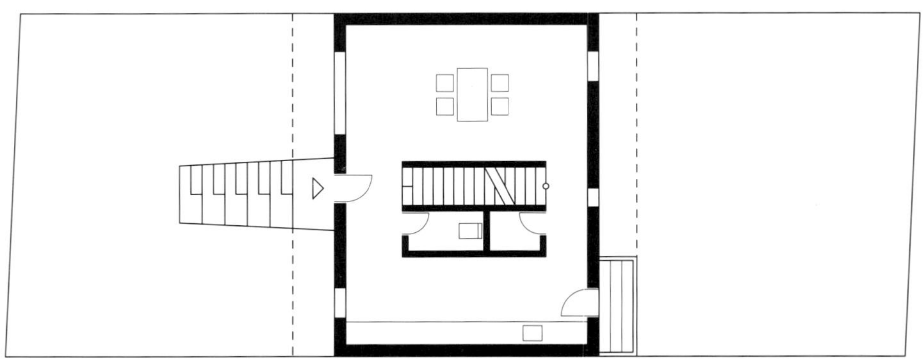

1st upper floor

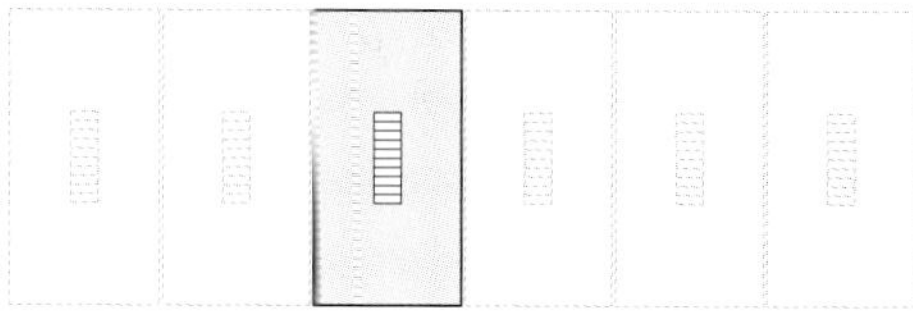

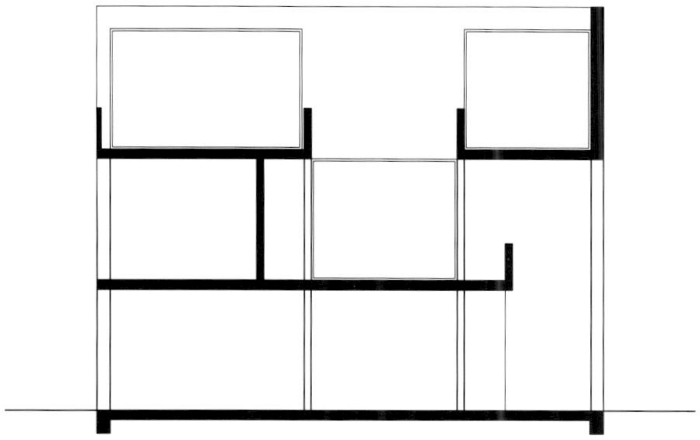

Longitudinal section

Longitudinal staircase
Three storeys
North-south orientation

This three-storey, north-south oriented house is defined and structured by a large south-facing terrace on the second floor that cuts deeply into the building volume. The terrace provides a small patio on the first floor as well as the rooms on the north side with south light. The patio can be covered with a glass roof; this would result in a small "energy garden" that could be used throughout the year. The dimensions of this house type can be modified and the open space above the dining area can be converted into a third personal room receiving south light. Another room could be created by converting the terrace on the third floor on the north side of the house. The terraces serve as secluded exterior spaces. Therefore, the garden on the ground level does not need to be further separated from the neighbouring gardens.

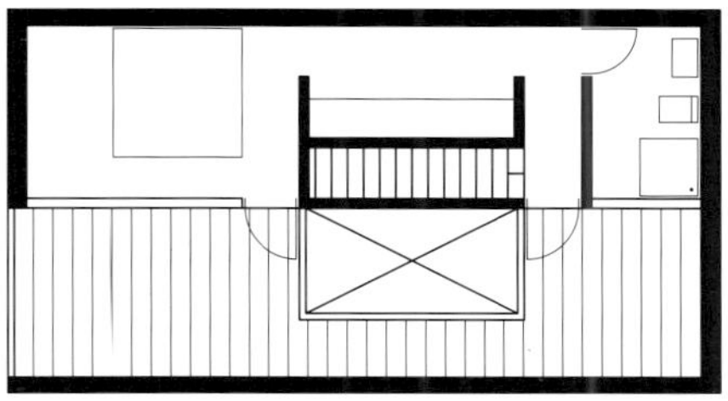

2nd upper floor

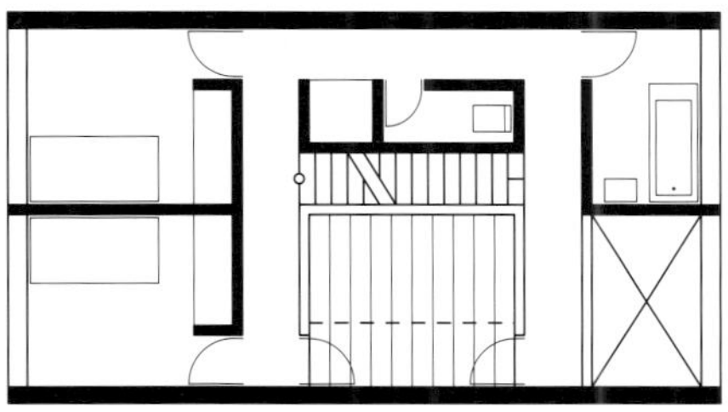

1st upper floor

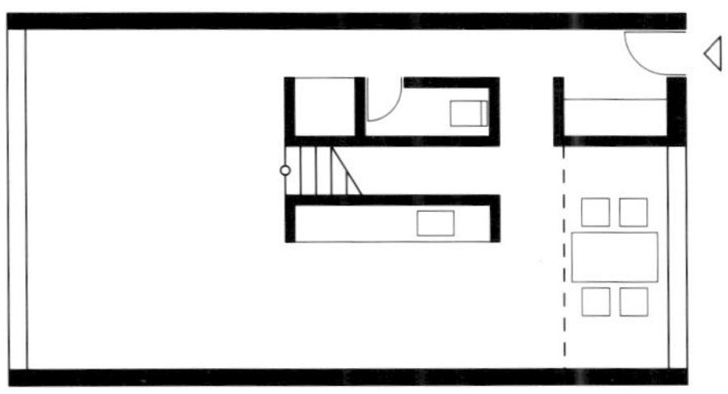

Ground floor

Student project
Darmstadt University
Leon Schmidt

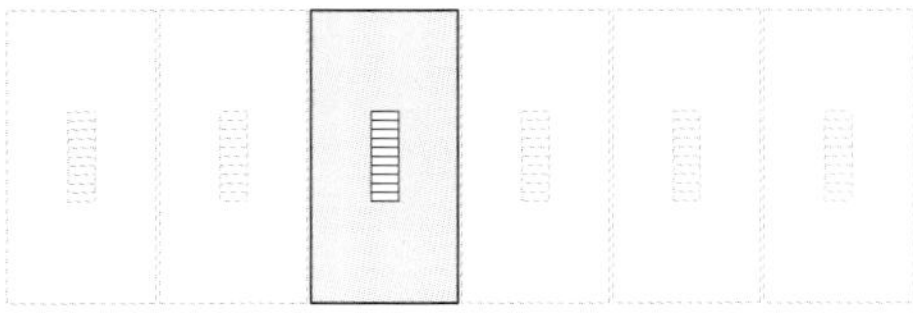

Longitudinal staircase
Three storeys
North-south orientation

This three-storey row house is arranged around a small two-storey atrium that provides additional daylight for the ground floor and opens out to a roof terrace on the upper floor. This house type is ideal for introverted use since the exterior spaces such as garden and forecourt are small. The floor plan allows for a free use of the space on the ground floor as well as for a variable position of the entrance. Depending on the dimensions of the building two or four rooms can be offered on the upper floor. A personal space on the top floor can accommodate an additional separate room, if desired. To include a basement, the staircase can be moved to the party wall. The roof terrace is closed off with trellises to provide a private exterior space. This house type offers sufficient privacy within an urban environment and can have any orientation.

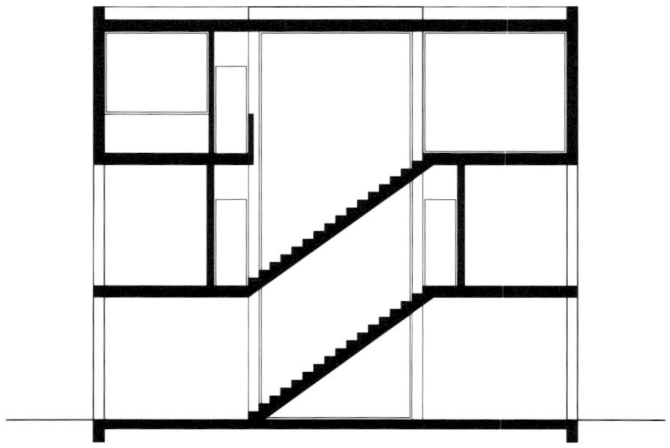

Longitudinal section

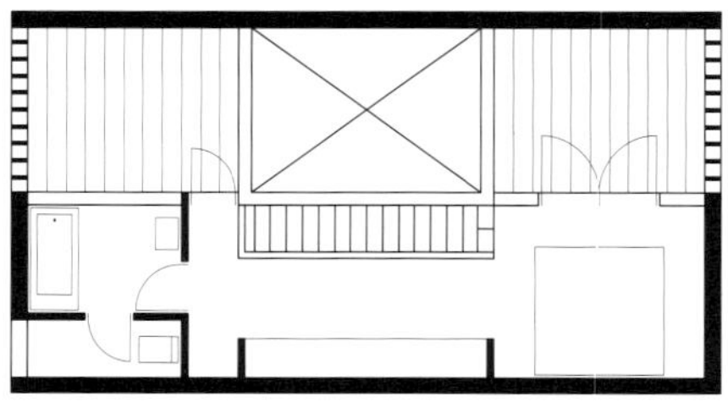

2nd upper floor

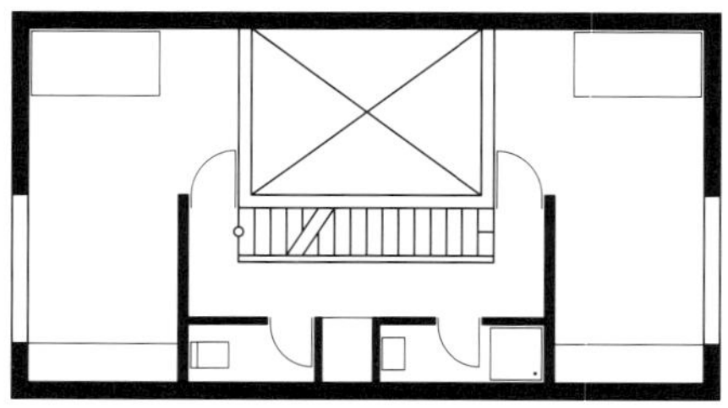

1st upper floor

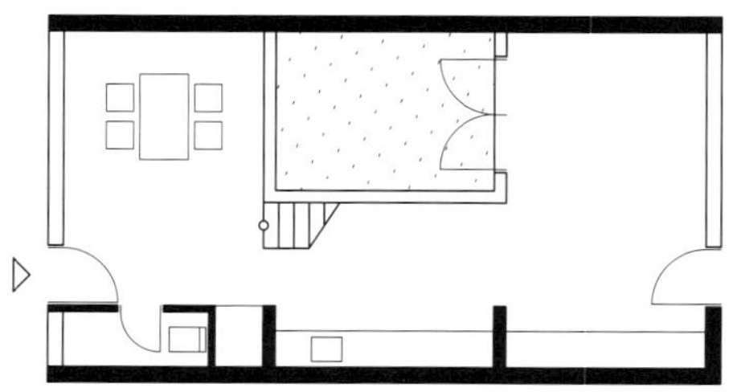

Ground floor

Student project
Darmstadt University
Simon Gallner

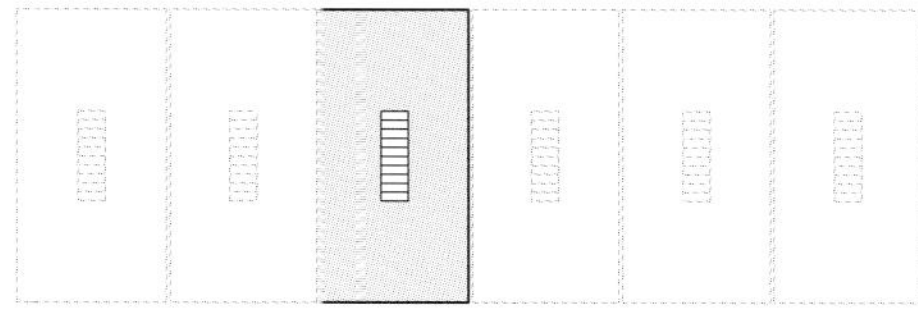

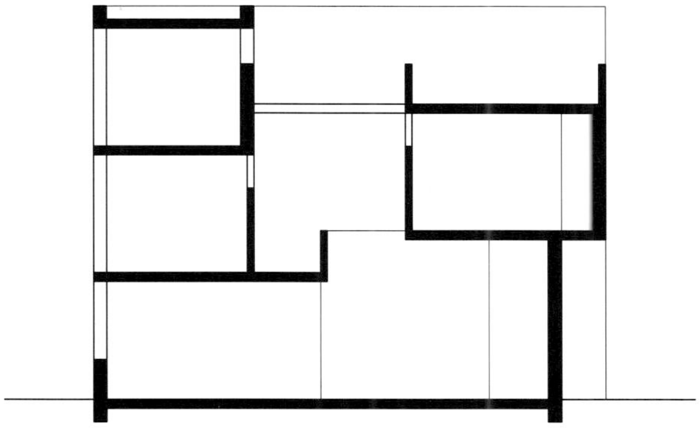

Longitudinal section

2nd upper floor

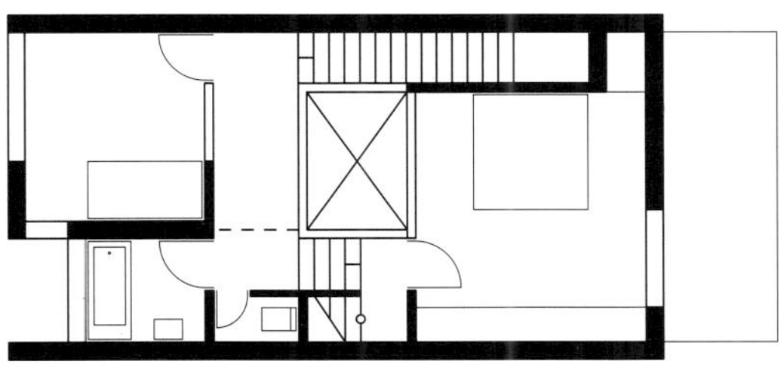

1st upper floor

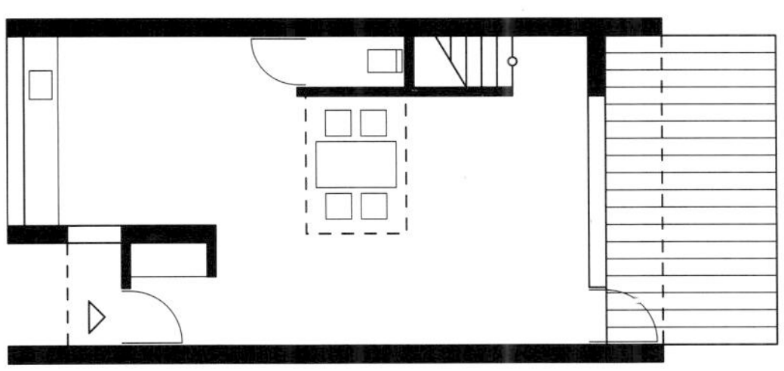

Ground floor

Longitudinal staircase
Three storeys
North-south orientation

The three-storey, north-south oriented row house features a small central atrium that extends through all storeys. This atrium provides the central ground floor area of the house with additional daylight and spatially connects all floors. In addition, the living space is higher than the other rooms; thus, the house has two storeys on the south side, whereas the north side features three storeys. The staggered arrangement of the levels and the central atrium provide the rooms on the north side with south light. From a typological viewpoint, this house type exemplifies that a sufficiently large interior open space not only expands the spatial experience of the building but also makes for plenty of daylight of the adjoining rooms. This can prove to be a major benefit within confined urban conditions. The location of the staircase landings on the first and top floor allows for easy linking with rooms of neighbouring units.

Student project
Darmstadt University
Markus Guenrigmann

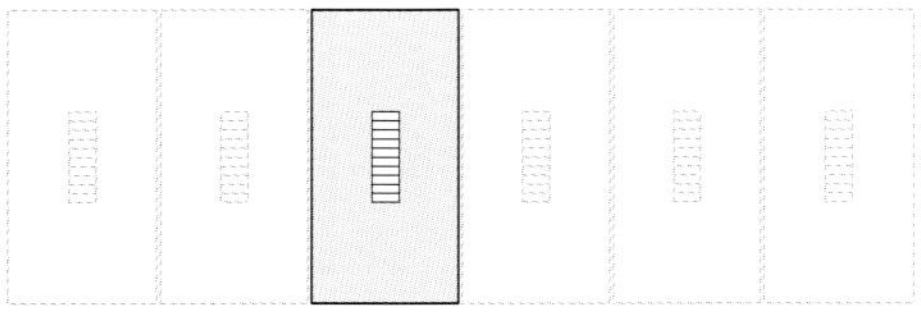

Longitudinal staircase
Three storeys
East-west orientation

The most notable characteristic of this three-storey row house is its long single-flight staircase, which is very attractive spatially and completely separated from all rooms. This element allows for a generously sized continuous living space on the ground floor free of any circulation zones. Access to the inner bathroom and the two rooms on the upper floor is provided for in the traditional manner by arranging it in the centre of the layout. On the second floor, the access zone opens out to the west side of the room, which extends across the entire storey and can be used as a second living space. On this level, separate personal rooms could only be realised with a long hallway – a disadvantage of this circulation system. The advantage of this house type is its capability to interlink with neighbouring units. The staircase could serve as access to a second house. In this case, cross-links between the two houses could be created on all levels, possibly with catwalks across the space above the staircase.

Group of houses "Voltstraat"
Tilburg, 1996
Rijnvos Voorwinde

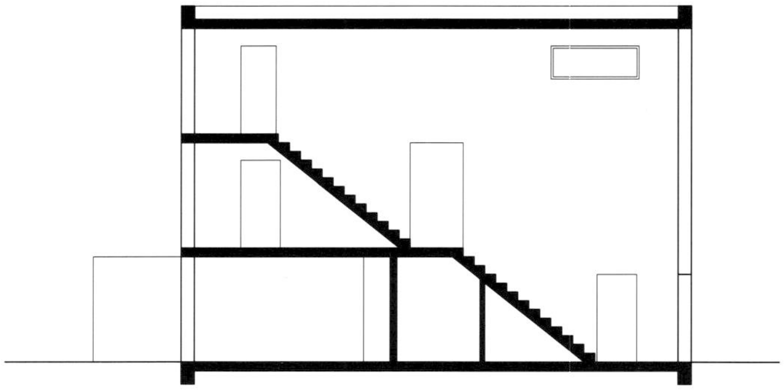

Longitudinal section

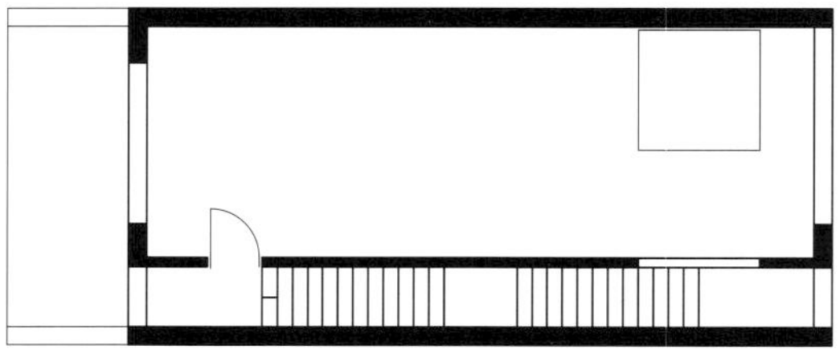

2nd upper floor

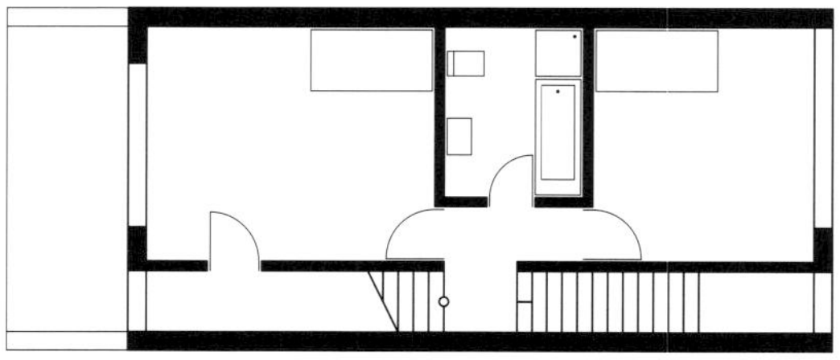

1st upper floor

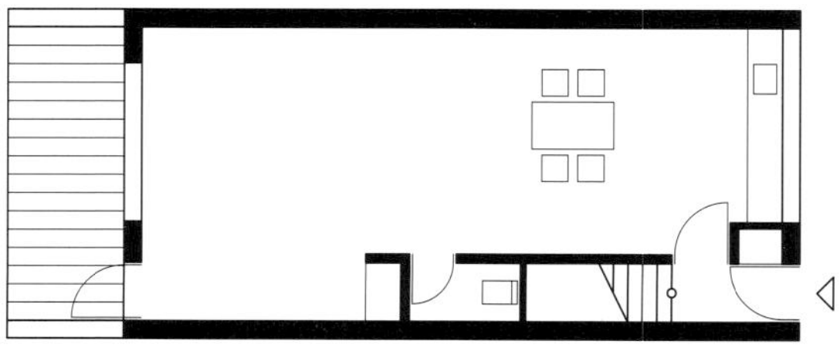

Ground floor

TE KOOP
12-NK-SL
RJ-TH-89

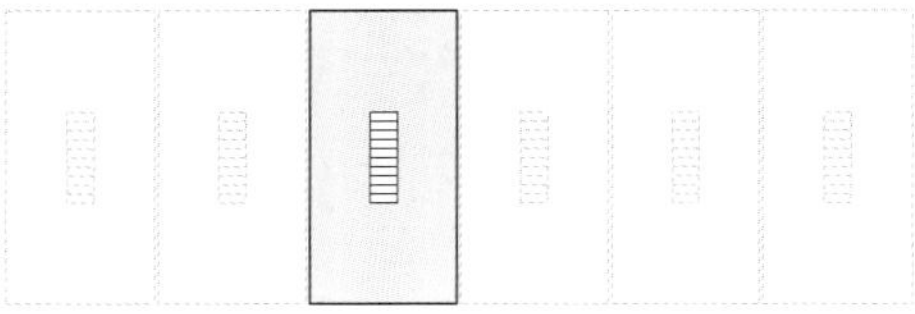

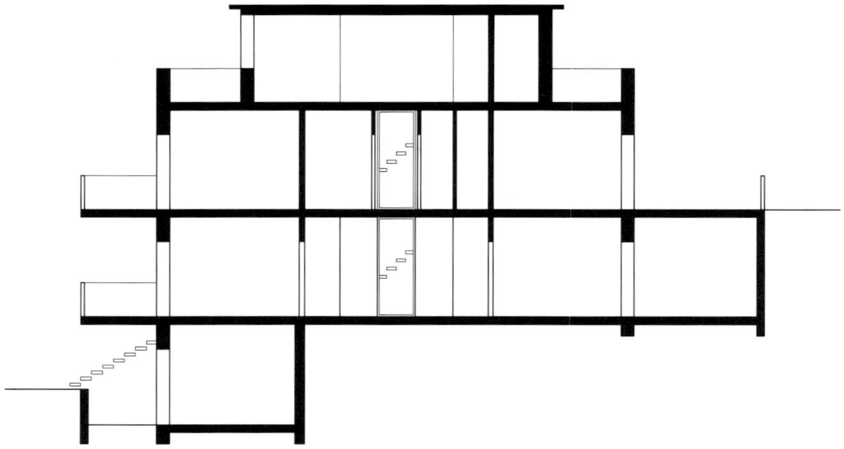

Longitudinal section

Longitudinal staircase
Three storeys
North-south orientation

A steeply inclined site is not mandatory for this house type. The clear differentiation between access zones and houses allows for a flexible interlinking with neighbouring units on every level. The ground floor features an open living and dining area with an inserted central block that accommodates service rooms. Personal rooms are located on the first floor. Due to the width of the house, two personal rooms on each side of the house can receive natural light. Since the garden's steep incline restricts its usability, the large roof terrace replaces the garden. The size of this house type is variable: the depth can be modified according to the topography and the width can be adapted to the arrangement of the rooms. The location of the staircase is advantageous when considering linking two neighbouring units. The internal zone on the first floor can be further optimised to integrate a kitchen with daylight. Because of the hillside topography only partial basements seem practical.

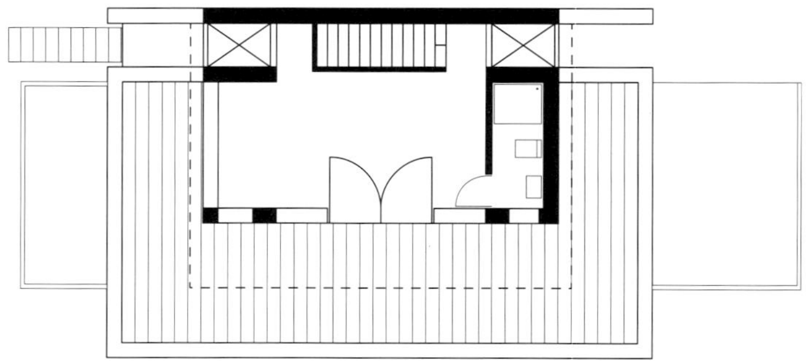

2nd upper floor

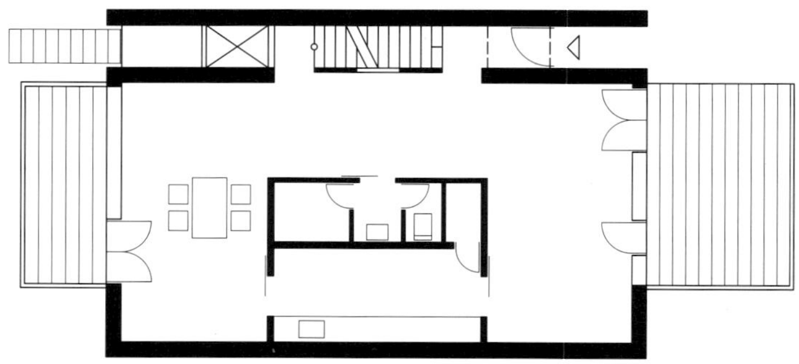

1st upper floor

Group of houses "Jagdgasse"
Innsbruck, 1999
Holzbox ZT

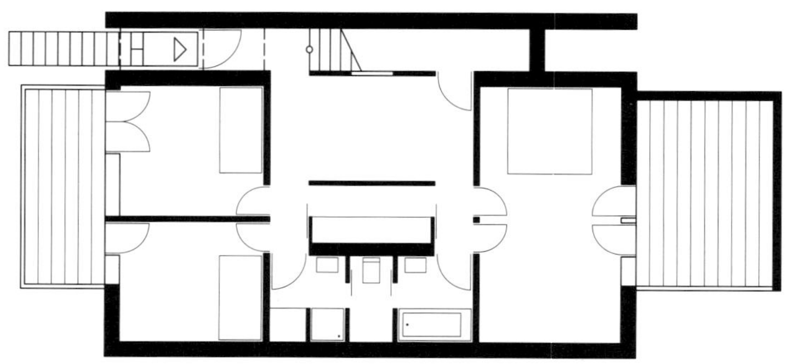

Ground floor

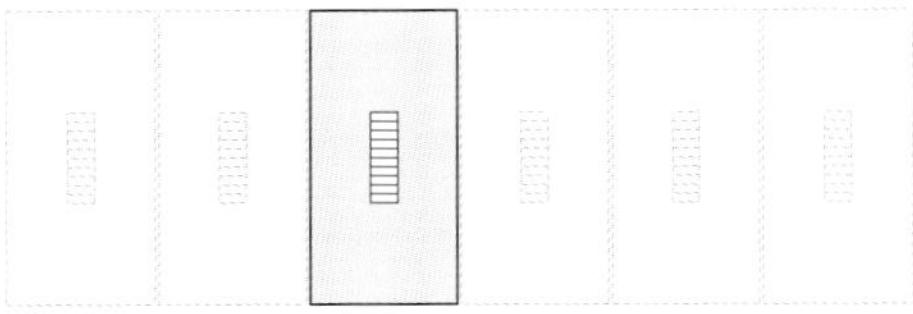

Longitudinal staircase
Three storeys
North-south orientation

Due to its inserted upper storey, this three-storey row house appears as an independent volume within its context and bears a resemblance to the individual character of a detached house. The differentiated structure of the building volume situated on a relatively large lot creates variegated open areas around the house. A roof terrace can be realised above the living space. The living area is generously dimensioned and the central location of the spiral staircase allows for economical access of the personal rooms on the upper levels. Since natural light is provided from all sides, this house type can be realised with virtually any orientation.
The disadvantages of this type are its large surface area in relation to its volume and a very limited flexibility in terms of adding units. In addition, the extreme layout of the personal rooms, specifically those on the first floor, restricts furnishing options.

Group of houses
Goirle, 1998
Bedaux de Brouwer

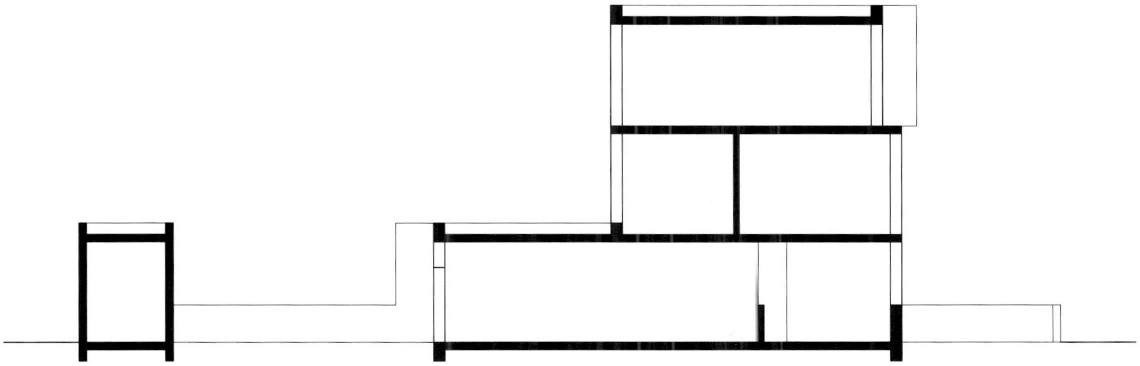

Longitudinal section

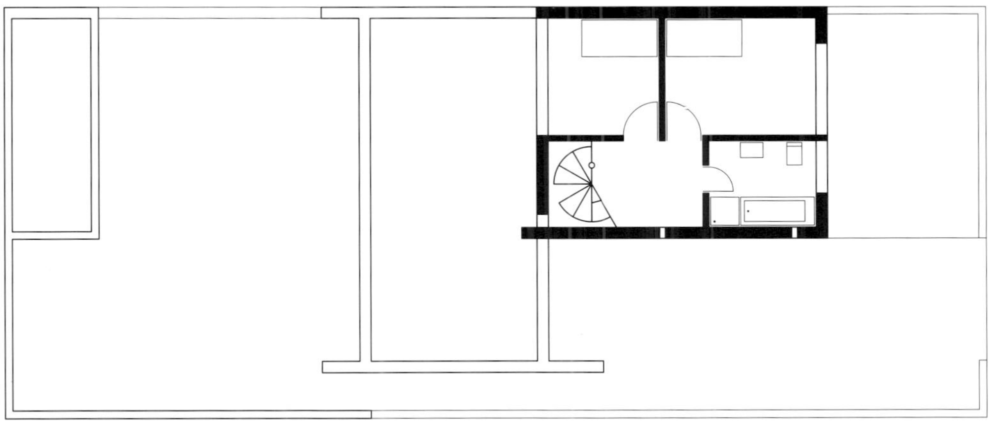

Upper floor

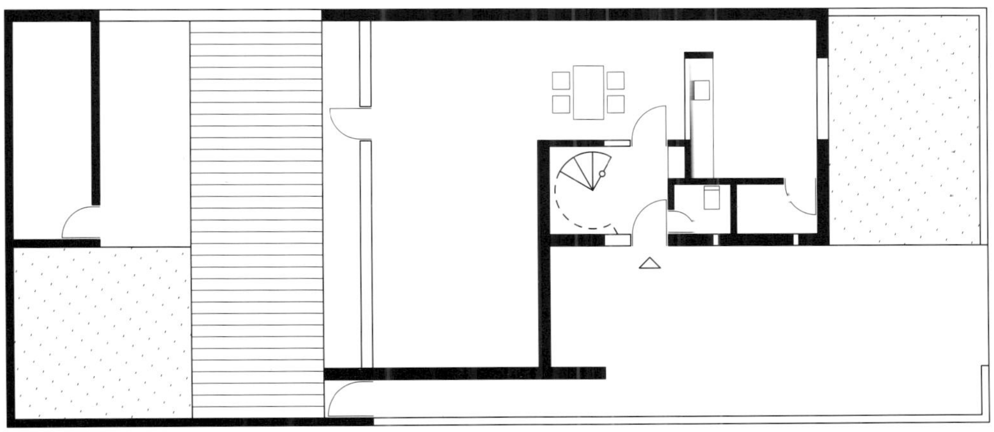

Ground floor

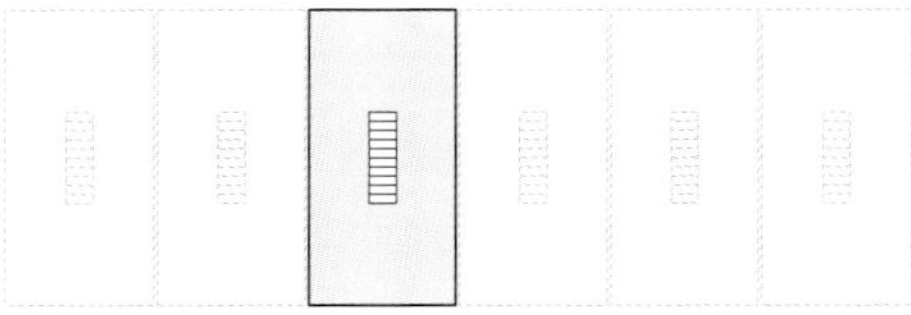

Longitudinal staircase
Three storeys
East-west orientation

The floor plan of this three-storey house is defined by its narrow width allowing only one room on every side. This results in a classic row house layout: the living room, facing west, is located on the ground floor, the kitchen is to be found in the centre of the house and the dining area is arranged near the entrance area on the front side of the house. On this side, a small exterior building volume for secondary uses shields the dining area from the public space. A single-flight staircase provides access to the upper levels and opens out to a large roof terrace which complements the open areas on the ground floor.
Each upper storey provides space for one or two separate personal rooms. In the floor plan shown here, the full number of possible rooms was traded off for a roof terrace and an open work area. The location of the landing staircase next to the party wall allows for easy modification of this house type by linking or separating individual rooms to or from the adjoining unit.

Group of houses "Quartier Mc Nair"
Berlin, 2000
d-company

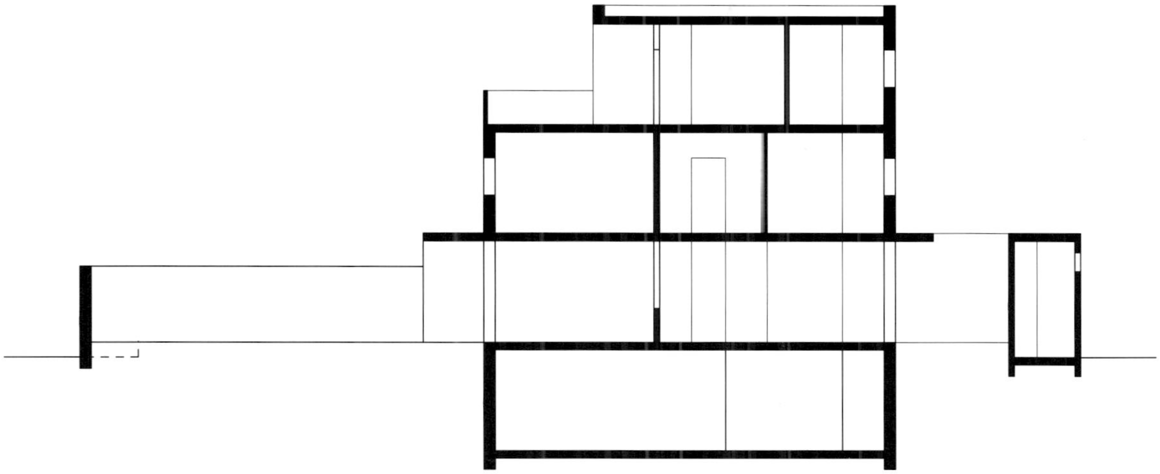

Longitudinal section

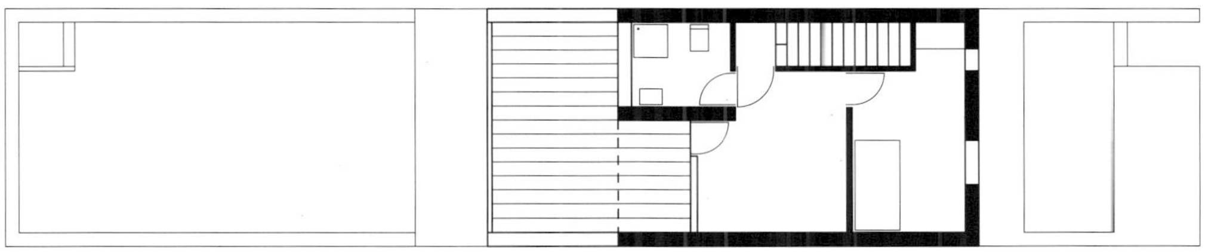

Top floor

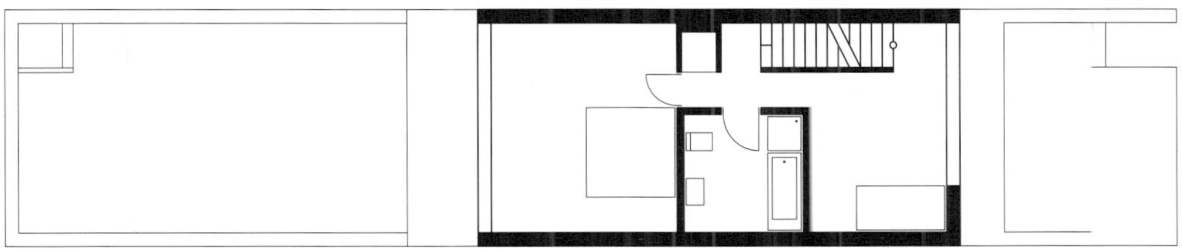

Upper floor

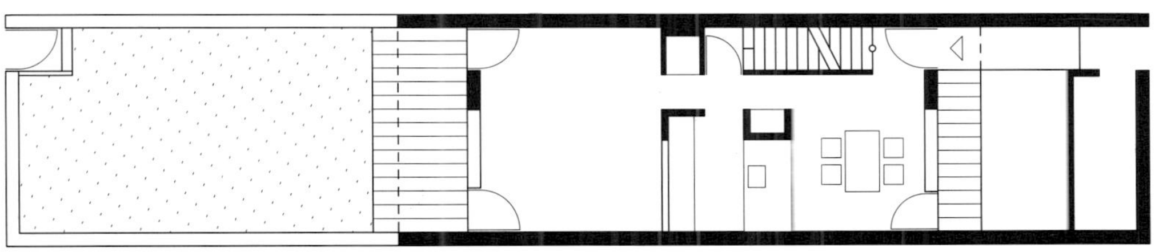

Ground floor

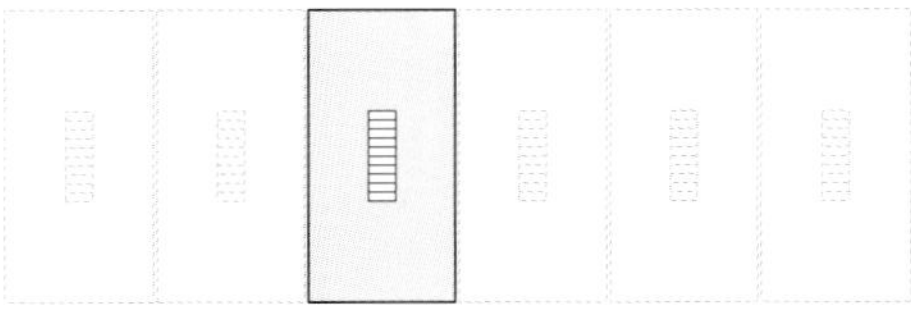

Longitudinal staircase
Three storeys
North-south orientation

The simple principle of positioning a front and a rear building on one lot is seldom used. However, it is ideally suited for specific forms of cohabitation (e.g. family house and parent's house). Whereas the two houses of this design have a rather conventional floor plan, the typologically characteristic feature lies in the combination of front and rear house. In this house type, the two-storey front-facing house accommodates a parking space and the pathway to the rear house on the ground level. The garden zone between the two houses is for joint use; which means that this area offers almost no secluded spaces. The living areas of the front building are located on the upper floor with terraces creating an outwardly orientation.
The bedrooms in both houses are on the top floor, whereby the roof of the higher building could be used as a roof terrace. This house type can be realised in various dimensions and variants as well as in reversed order.

Project "Wachsendes Haus"
Berlin, 1999
schneider+schumacher

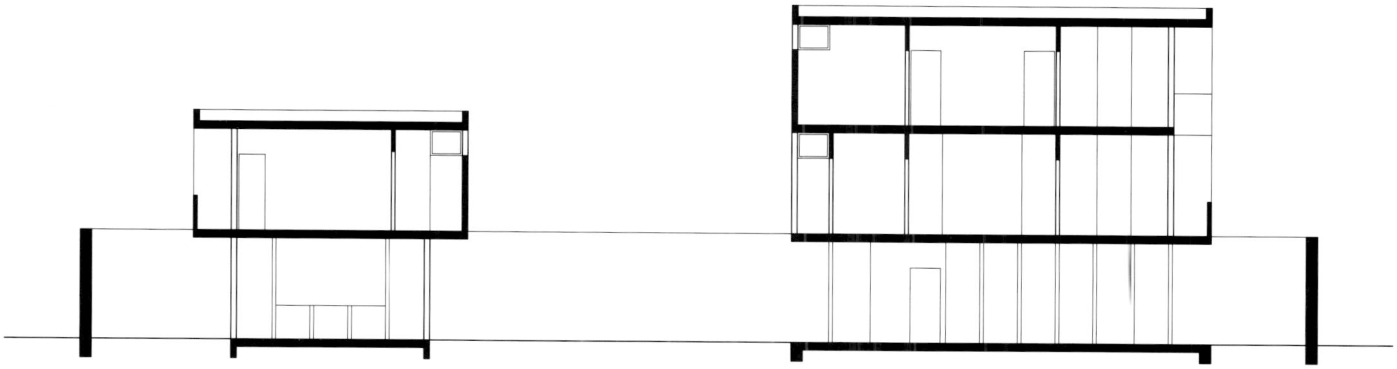

Longitudinal section

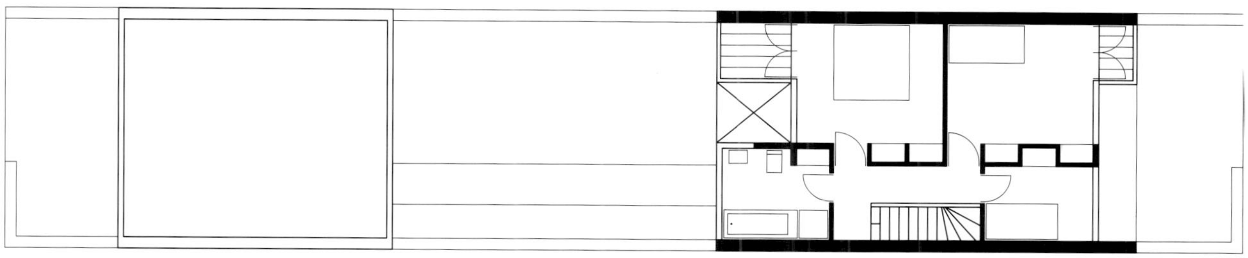

2nd upper floor

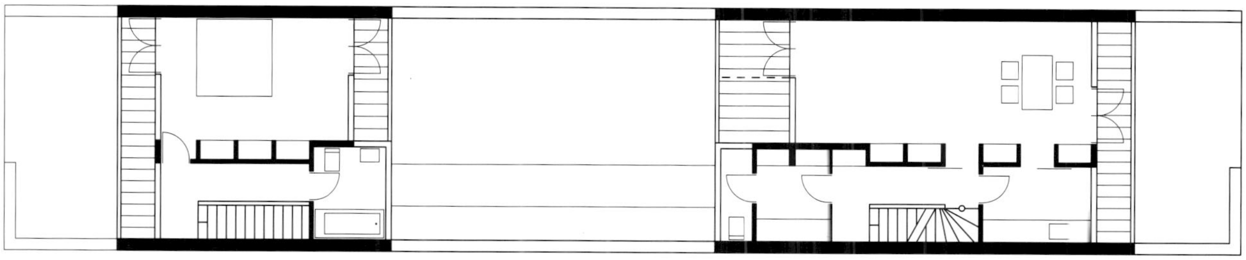

1st upper floor

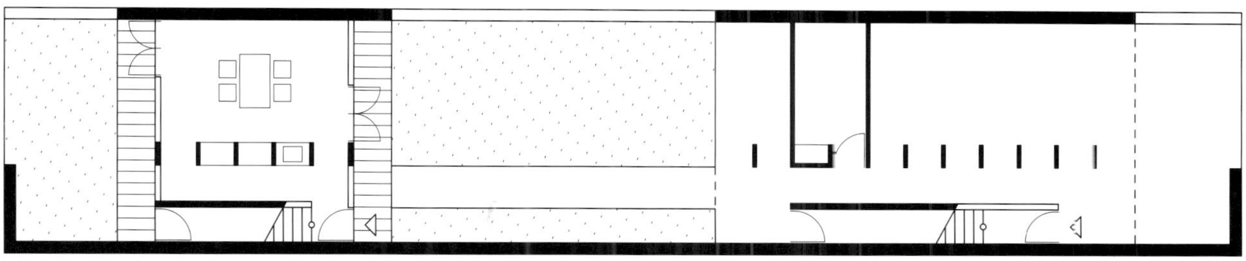

Ground floor

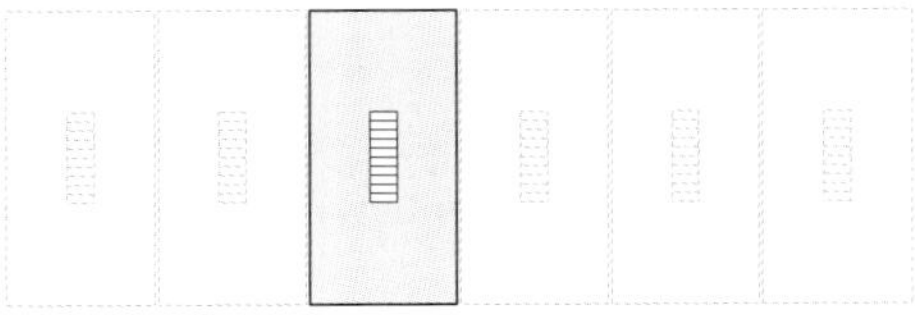

Longitudinal staircase
Three storeys
East-west orientation

Typologically, this housing unit is not really a row house but a multi-family house with duplexes in a row on the upper floor. The apartments on the ground floor are more or less conventional; their layout follows that of typical multi-storey houses. The upper floor of this house type is accessed via a single-flight staircase leading into a broad central hallway. The generously dimensioned corridor almost resembles a residential street and features natural light. From here the flats are entered. On this level, they comprise two personal rooms that are lit from one side as well as a bathroom and a separate toilet. A double-flight staircase leads to the top floor, which accommodates living areas that are oriented towards two sides, and a roof terrace. The switch from a one-sided to a double-sided orientation is achieved by reducing the space of the flats on the top floor to only one building axis whereas on the first floor they extend across two axes. The result is a complex interwoven arrangement of dwellings with orientations to all sides.

Group of houses
Fussach, 2000
baumschlager & eberle

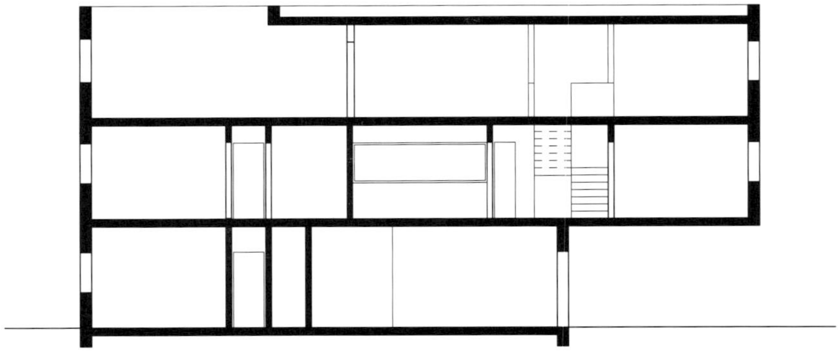

Cross section

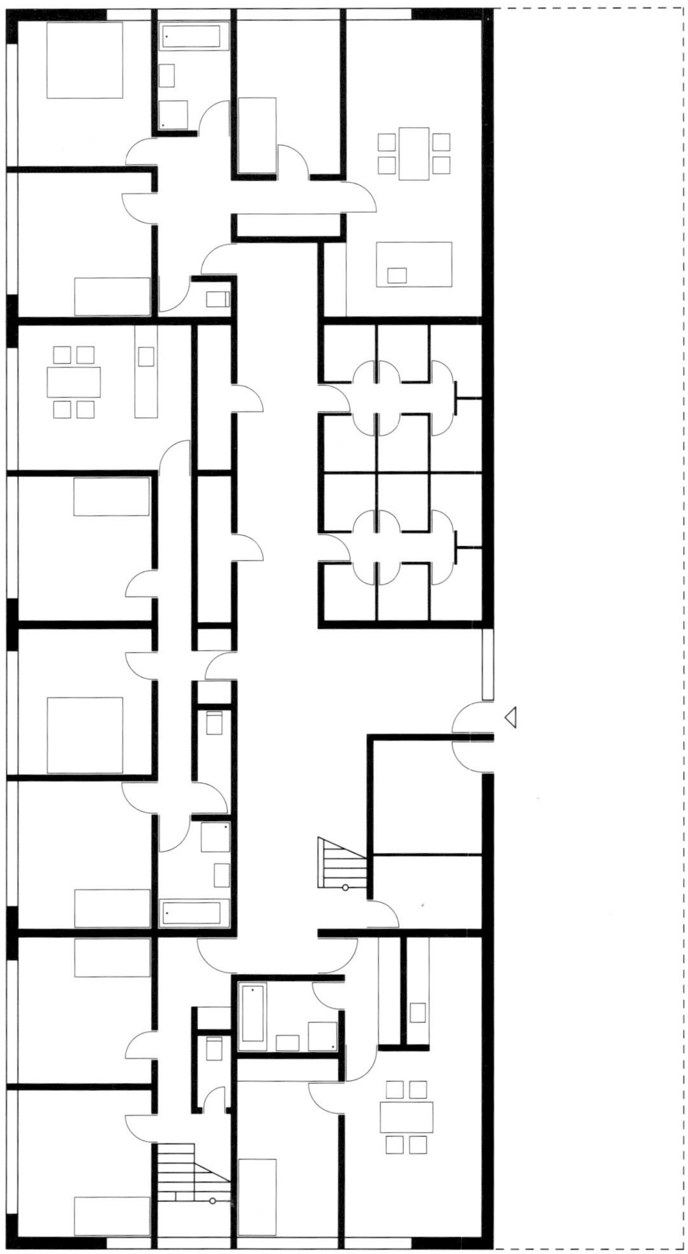

Ground floor

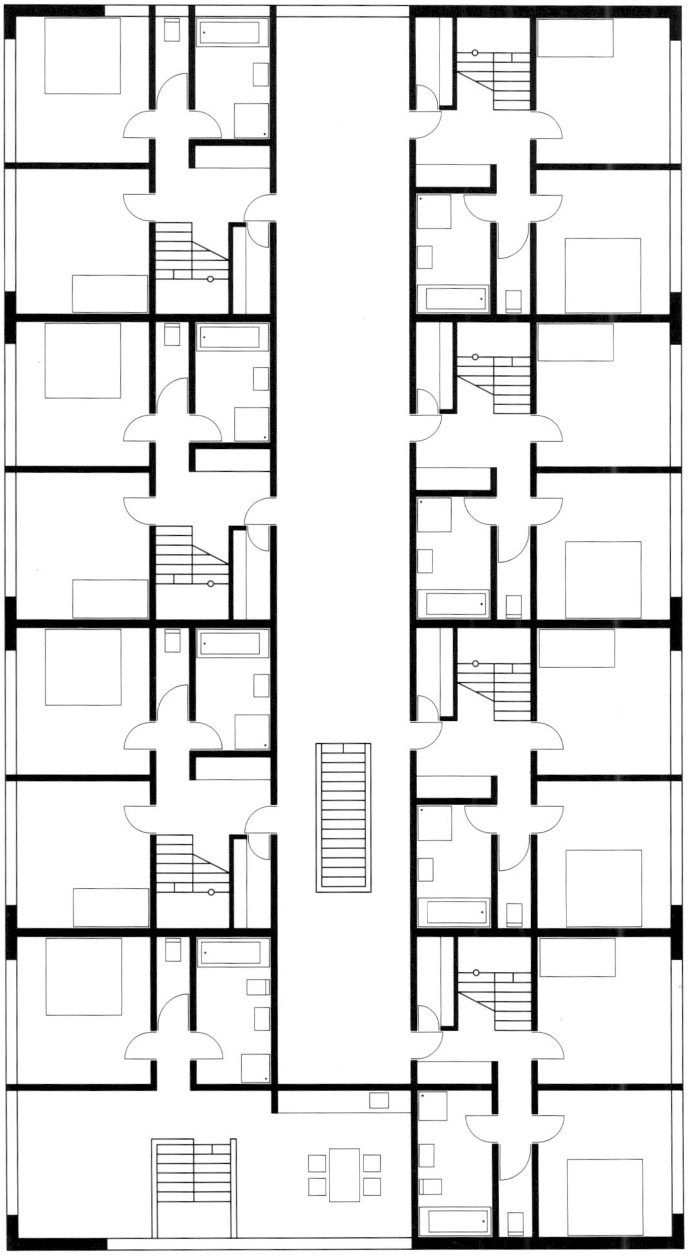

1st upper floor

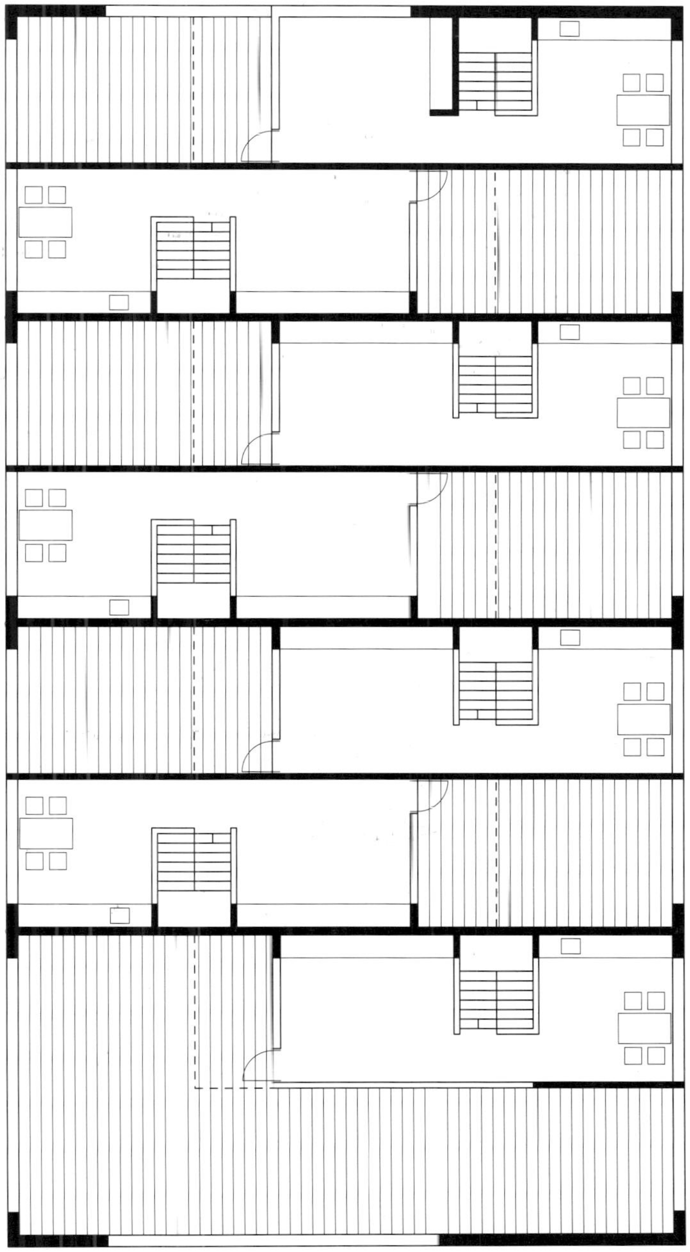

2nd upper floor

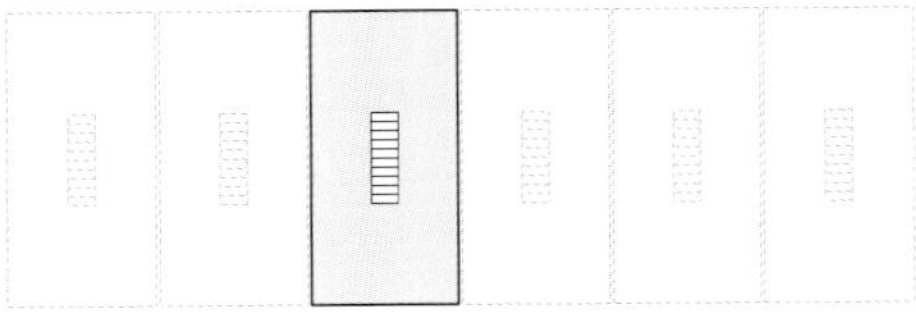

Longitudinal staircase
Four storeys
North-south orientation

Four-storey row houses are well suited to urban properties offering little open space. This type is characterised by its two-sided access, the two-storey open space with a mezzanine and a roof terrace above.
The ground floor houses a parking space and a personal room that can also be used by other parties. The first floor comprises a large double-height room, which can serve as a living space or studio, and another personal room. A third personal room is located on the third floor, as is the roof terrace providing a private exterior space. A bathroom is to be found only on the first floor – a disadvantage considering that three storeys are being served by it. The staircase does not receive any daylight and is rather narrow compared to the generously dimensioned rooms. Variable uses of the different levels are typical for this type of building. Even a complete separation of storeys including separate access is possible.

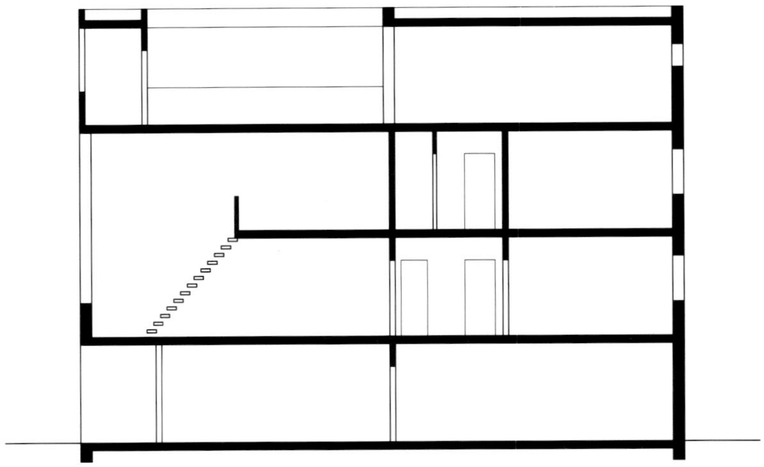

Longitudinal section

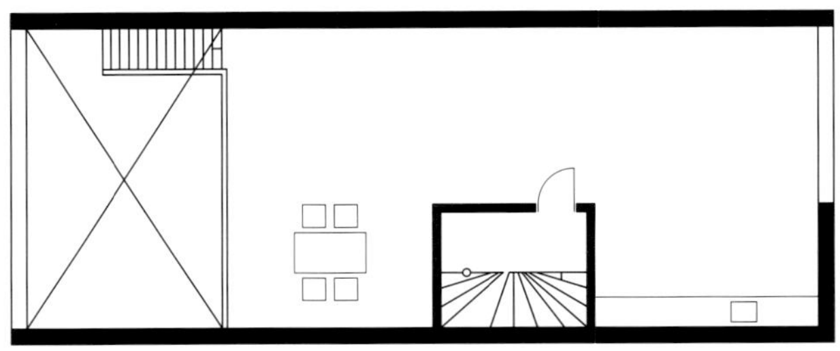

2nd upper floor

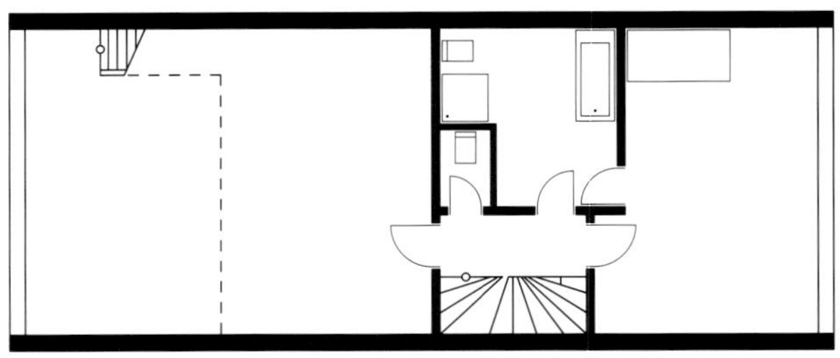

1st upper floor

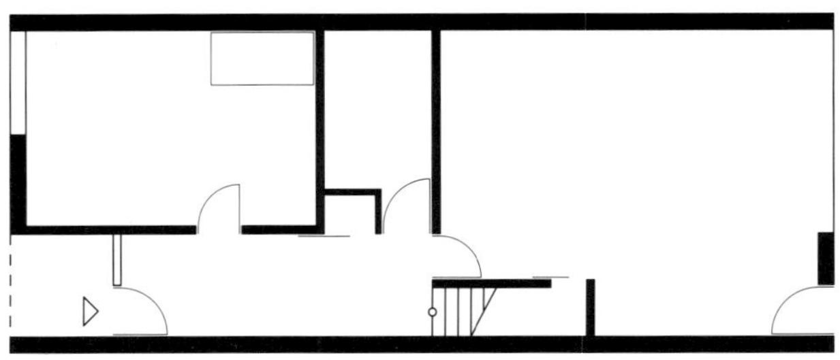

Ground floor

Group of houses "De Landtong"
Rotterdam, 1997
Frits van Dongen

RN-ZH-35

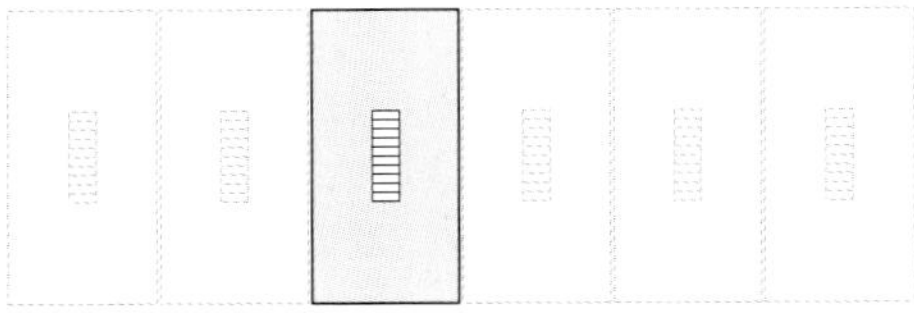

Longitudinal staircase
Four storeys
North-south orientation

This four-storey house comprises two row houses, one stacked above the other. The two houses are accessed via an exter or single-flight staircase that extends across two storeys and determines the width of the building as well as the length of the narrower part of the floor plan. The lower house can be accessed either from the first floor or from the ground floor. The ground floor could also be used independently as a workspace directly accessible from the street. The upper house is accessed via the second floor. Interior circulation is provided by a single-flight staircase, which is always located in the wider building part.
The open spaces within the structures let sunlight reach far into the building. The areas in the centre of the houses are used as bathrooms and kitchens. This type is defined by the length of the staircase. Its width can be modified and it can be interlinked with adjoining units to create several flats of variable size.

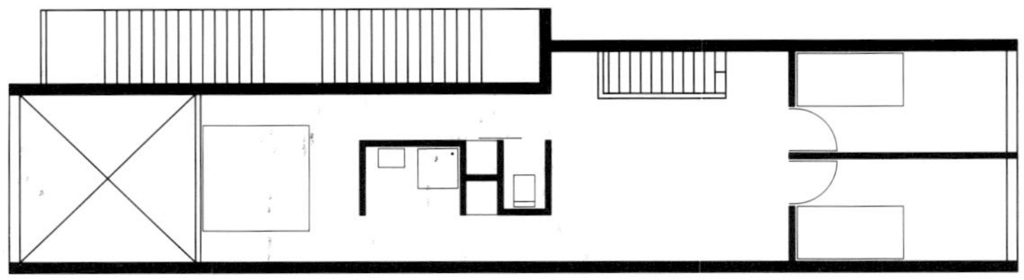

3rd upper floor

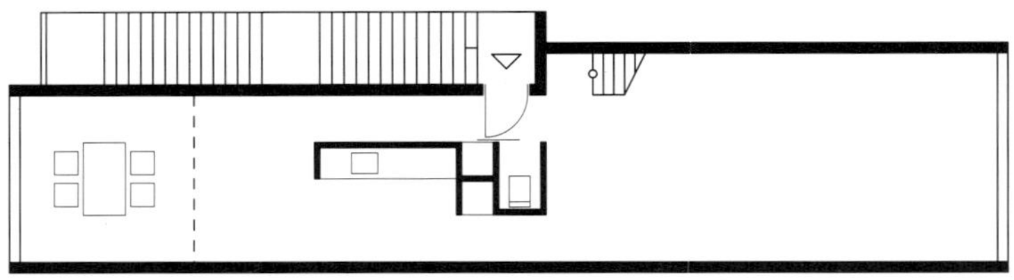

2nd upper floor

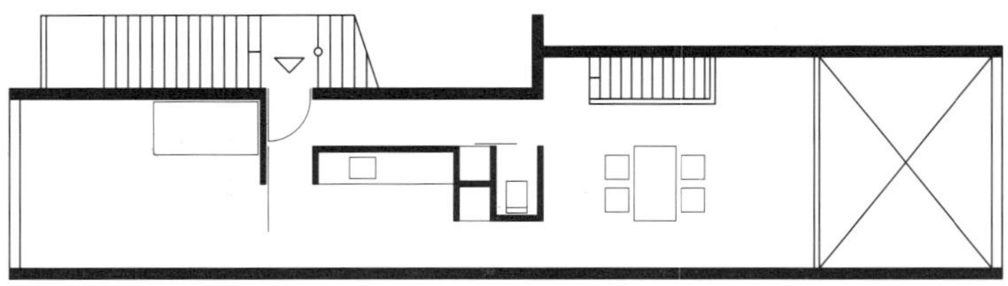

1st upper floor

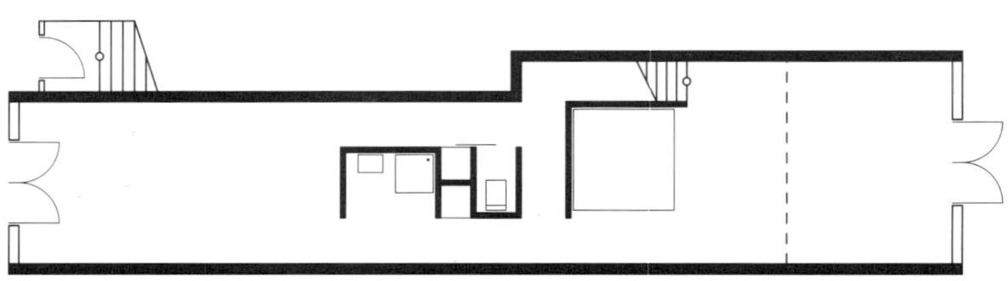

Ground floor

28 apartments
Amsterdam, 1994
Bosch Haslett

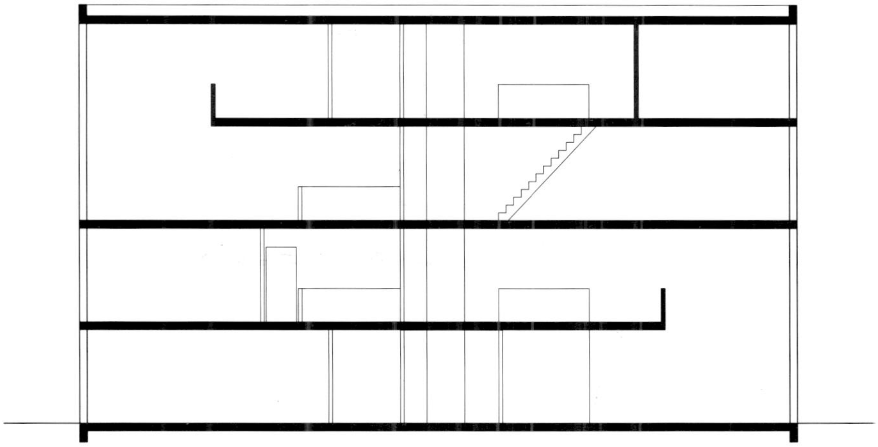

Longitudinal section

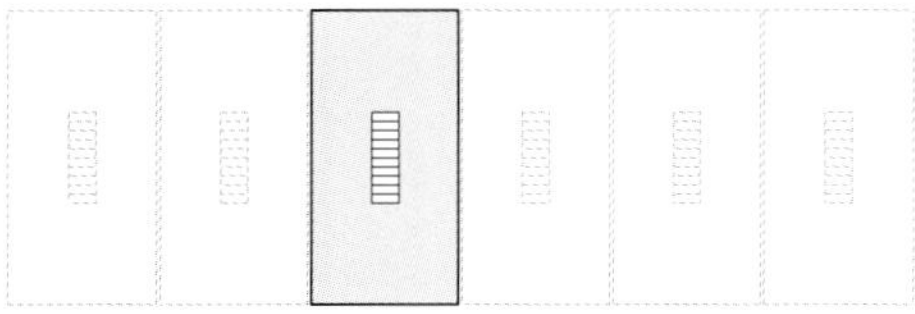

Longitudinal staircase
Four storeys
North-south orientation

The key characteristic of this narrow house type is the longitudinal division of the floor plan. This makes the already narrow proportions of the space even more extreme. The apparently illogical design approach reveals its qualities when the possibilities for daylighting and the dramaturgy of the spatial experience are considered. Dividing the floor plan lengthwise allows full-height glazing of the rooms without permitting insights from the outside. This creates the impression of a completely open glasshouse amidst dense urban developments. In the upper storeys, two closed jutties extend into the open space above the courtyard; they contrast with the open areas and therefore enhance the spatial concept. The entrance to the house is located on a mezzanine level. Going downstairs, one enters the eat-in-kitchen; upstairs, the long room comprises the living spaces. Personal rooms are located in the niche-like cubes attached to the long room.

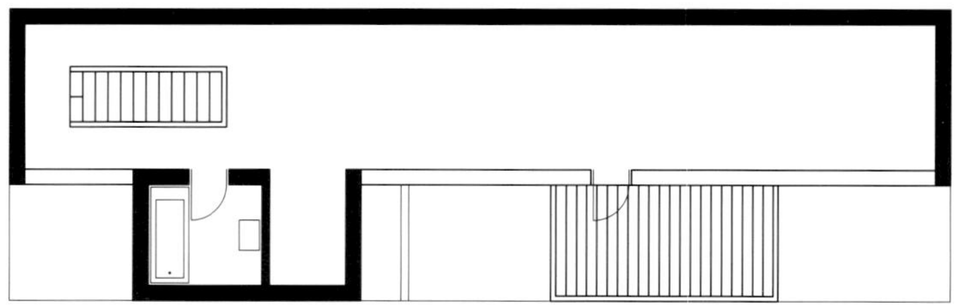
3rd upper floor

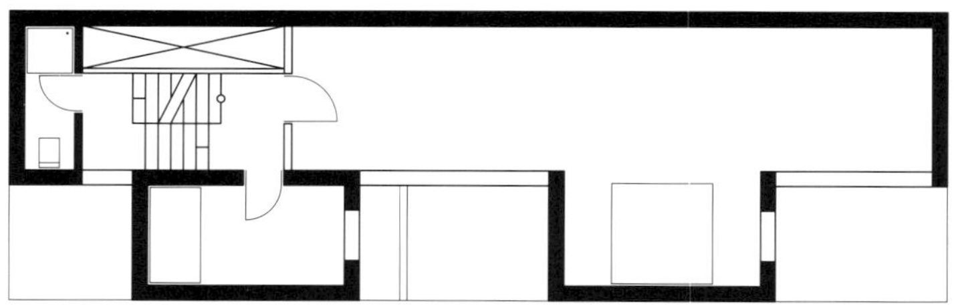
2nd upper floor

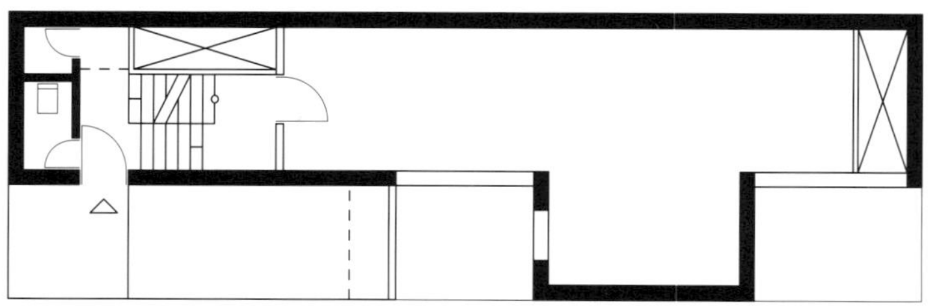
1st upper floor

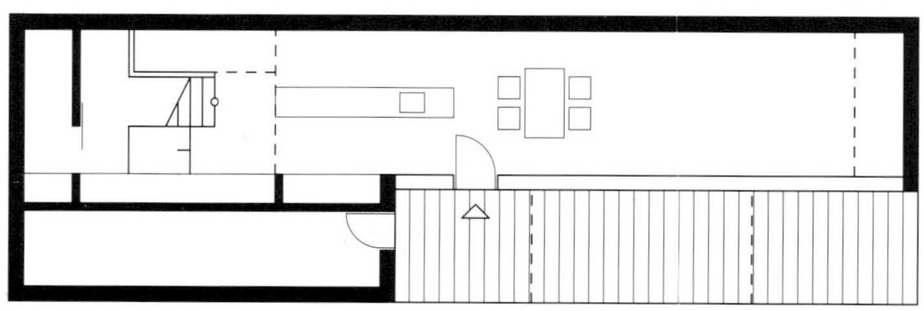

Ground floor

"Scheepstimmermanstraat" house
Amsterdam, 1999
MVRDV

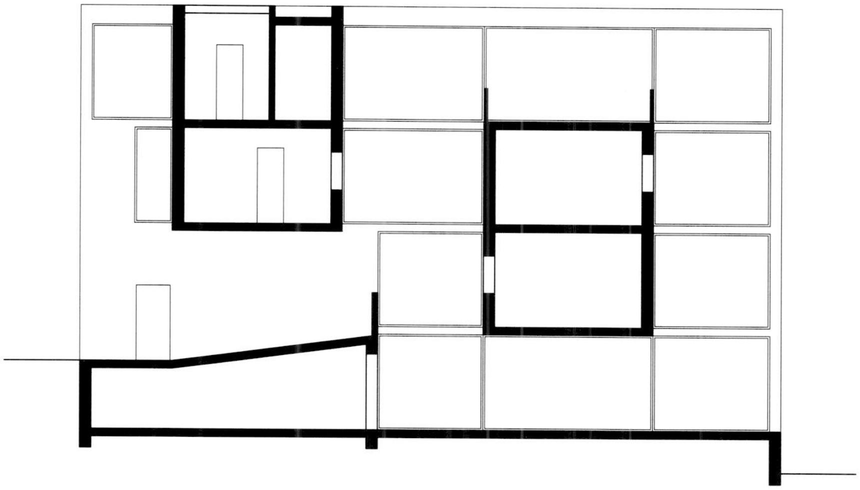

Longitudinal section

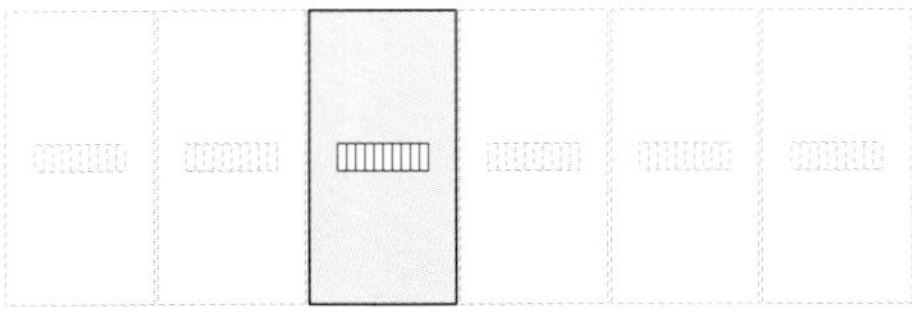

Transversal staircase
Two storeys
North-south orientation

In this small south-facing row house, all living spaces are arranged on one side. Circulation areas on the north side are kept to a minimum. The user can organise the kitchen, dining area and living room on the ground floor according to his needs. Three personal rooms are located on the first floor. Removable partition walls and a construction of the exterior wall providing options to connect to partition walls create variable room dimensions. High walls protect the open space from neighbouring houses. Storage rooms and a small terrace are located towards the rear of the garden. The dimensions of this house are completely variable. It can be designed to be deeper, higher or wider, and the rooms can be modified accordingly. However, the house must be oriented to the south. The method of construction can also be modified.

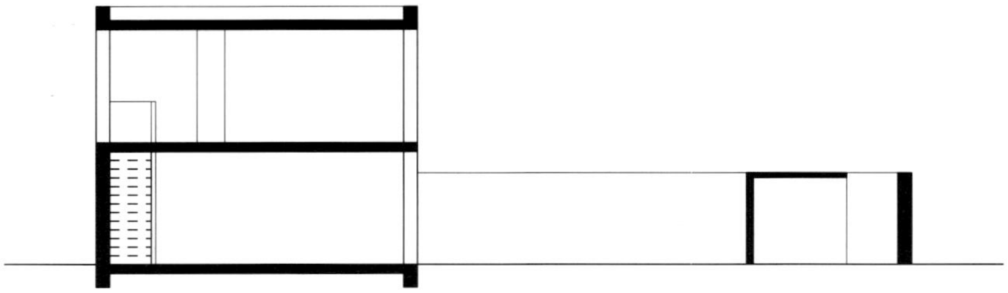

Longitudinal section

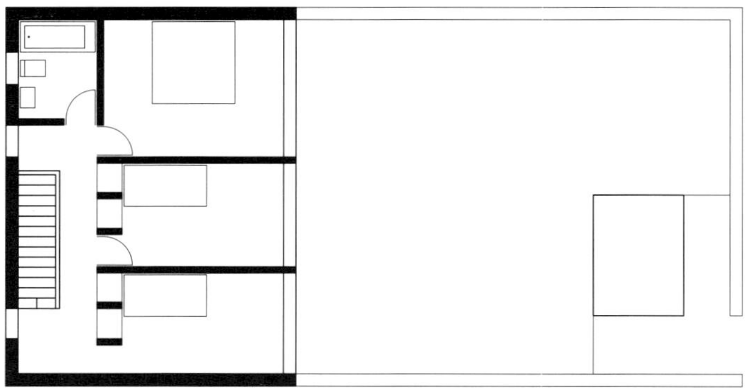

Upper floor

Project "Karower Damm"
Berlin, 1999
Rolf Mühlethaler

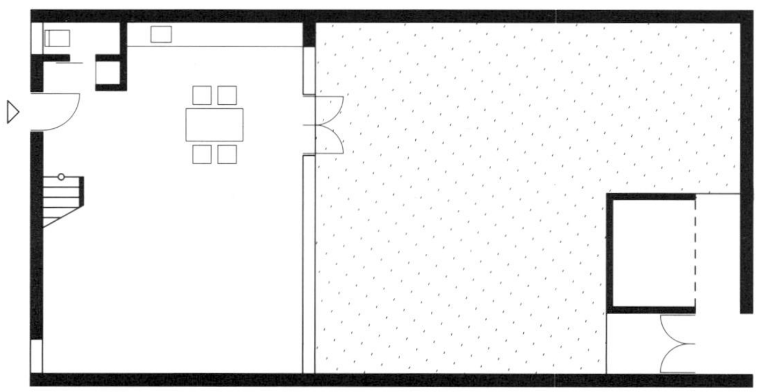

Ground floor

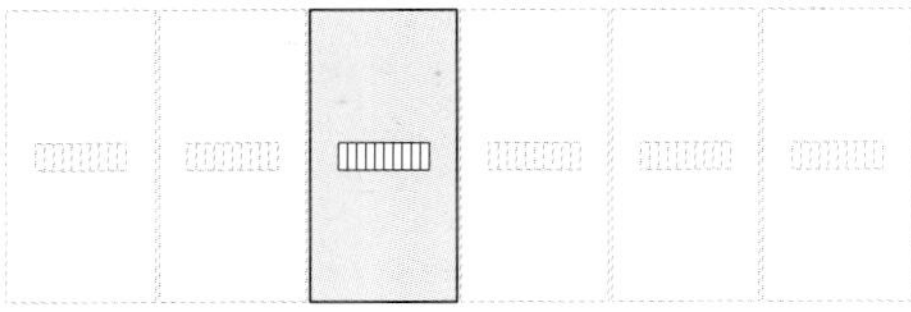

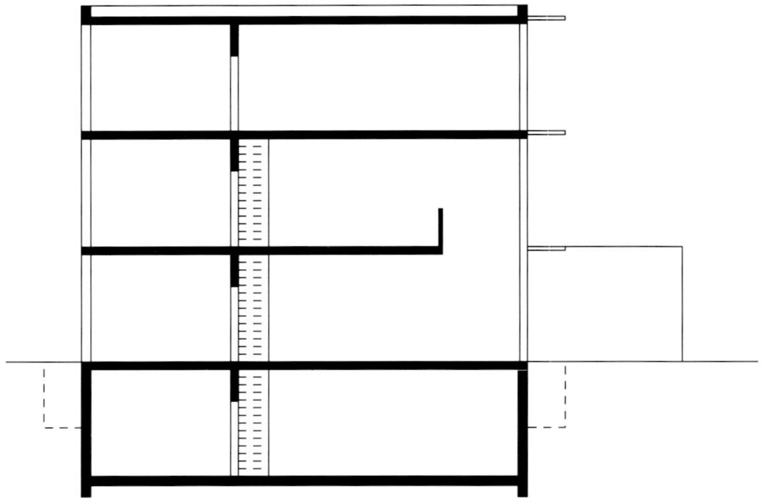

Longitudinal section

Transversal staircase
Three storeys
North-south orientation

The simplest form of a row house still is the house type with a single-flight staircase running crosswise, dividing the house into two zones comprising on the entrance level, facing north, the entrance area and kitchen, and bathroom and personal rooms on the other levels. In this case, the first floor is a mezzanine which constitutes a spatial extension of the ground floor. A large play or work area is located on the second floor in front of the personal rooms.
This house type is highly modifiable. A two-storey structure makes for a simple house with three personal rooms. The three-storey version can comprise additional rooms or a roof terrace. The width of the house is variable; however, the length of the staircase has to be considered. A south-facing orientation as shown is beneficial, but west or east orientations have only little negative impact.

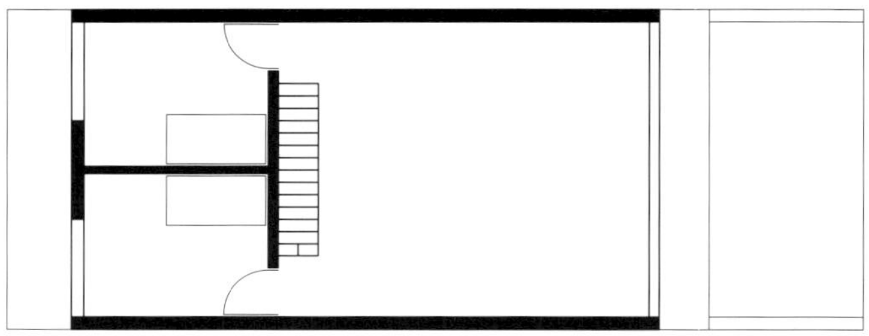

2nd upper floor

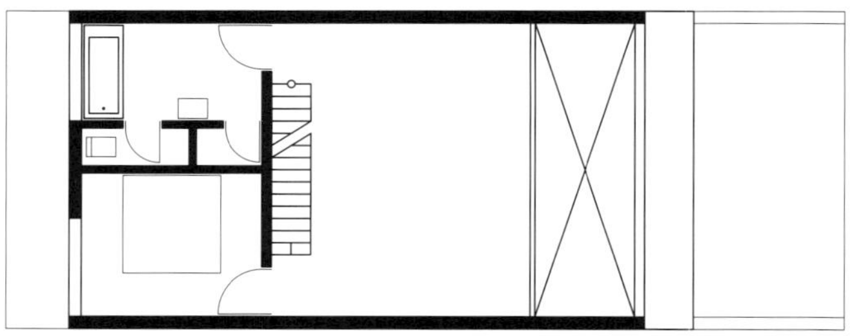

1st upper floor

Residential park at Betzenberg
Kaiserslautern, 2000
AV 1

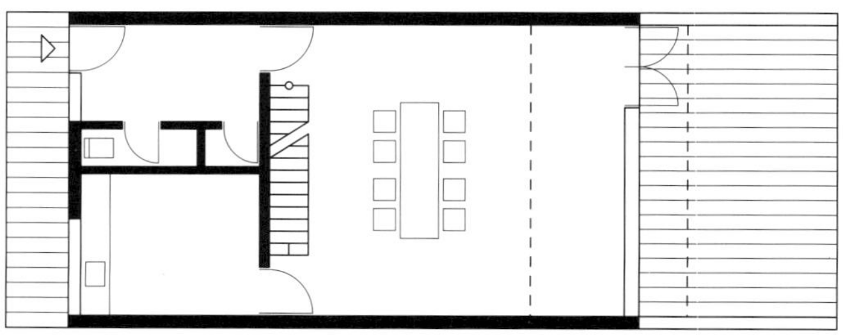

Ground floor

FLOOR

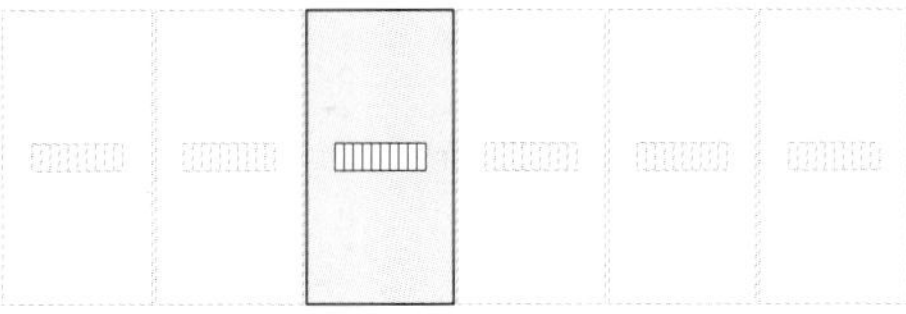

Transversal staircase
Three storeys
North-south orientation

This small house type with a landing staircase in the centre is a good example that economical construction on a very small site is possible without spatial deficits. A parking space is integrated into the house on the ground floor and entry level. A landing staircase leads to a protruding living room half a level down, which spatially is connected to the eating area and kitchen. A courtyard on the south-west side of the living room provides a protected open space. Sufficiently large children's rooms and a bathroom are located on the first floor. The second floor with the third personal room is linked to a south-facing roof terrace, which can also be developed into a room, if desired. The protruding living room can be realised in different sizes since the courtyard alongside allows an expansion towards the south. This house type can also be arranged in an east-west orientation.

Drive-in row houses
Amsterdam, 1995
Geurst & Schulze

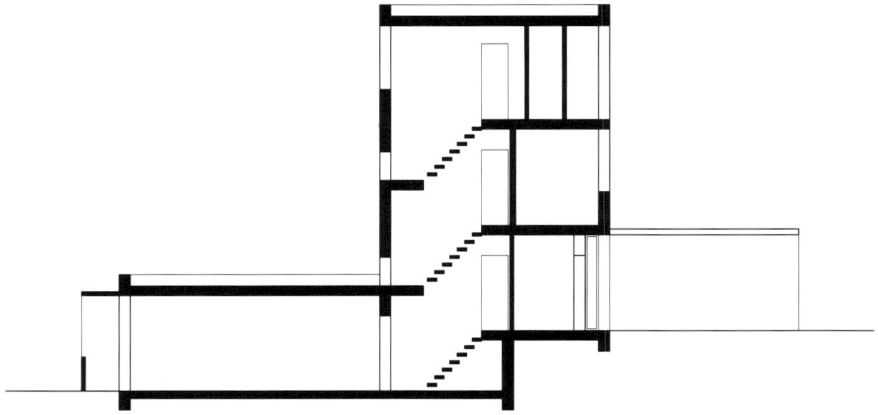

Longitudinal section

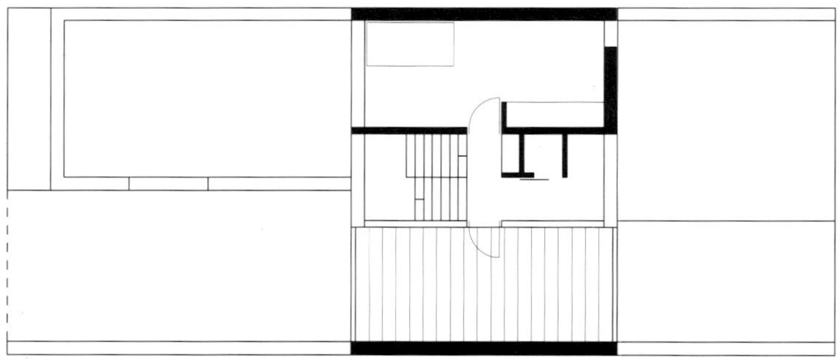

2nd upper floor

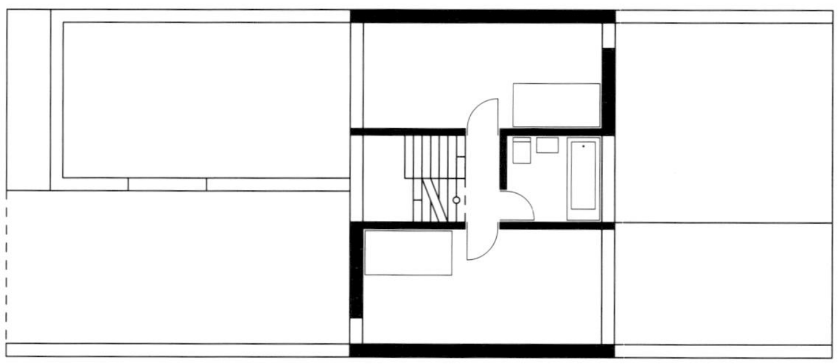

1st upper floor

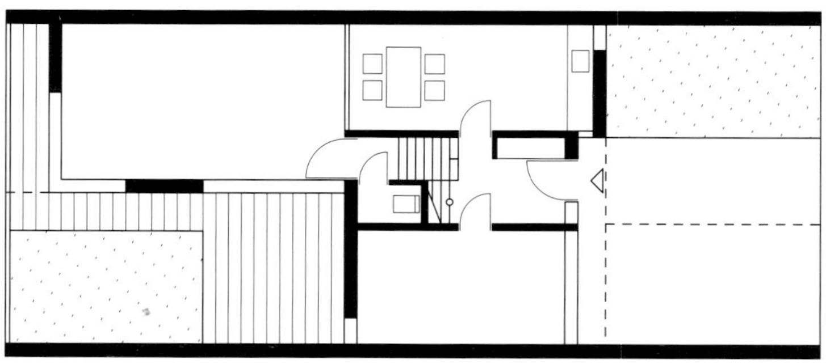

Ground floor

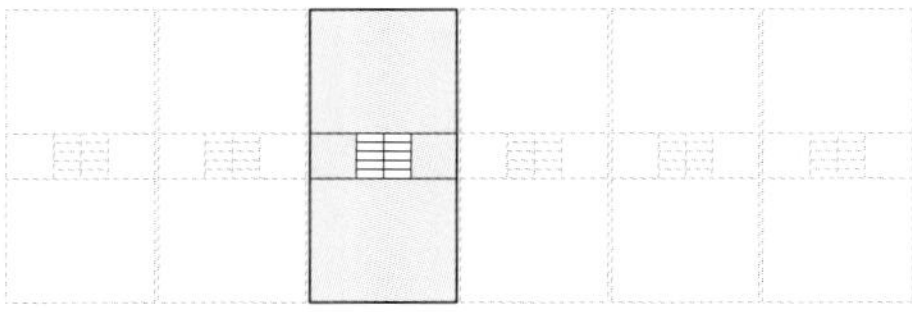

Longitudinal split-level
Three storeys
East-west orientation

This split-level house type is characterised by its intelligent embedding into the topography. As a result, only two of the three storeys are visible from the outside. The living area is located half a level above the garden level. The personal rooms in the half-basement also have access to the garden via an exterior staircase. A void providing daylight and airiness extends from the living level up to the roof terrace and gives this small house the feeling of a generously dimensioned space. The personal room on the first floor opens up to the void via an interior glazing. The roof terrace is treated as an exterior room and offers a secluded open space. This house can be designed with a narrower floor plan if one of the personal rooms in the half-basement is eliminated. In this case, the bathroom on the upper floor replaces part of the open space above the living area. Due to the void, the bedroom on the upper floor is well-lit and does not necessarily require a window.

Residential park at Kirchhölzle
Schopfheim, 1990
Günter Pfeifer

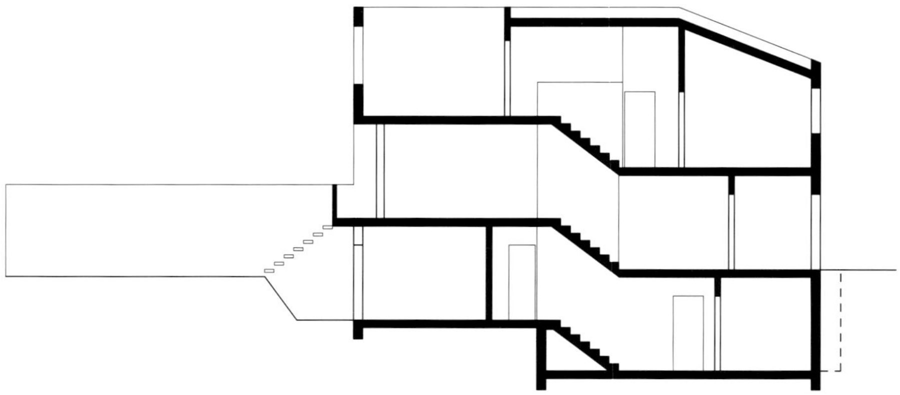

Longitudinal section

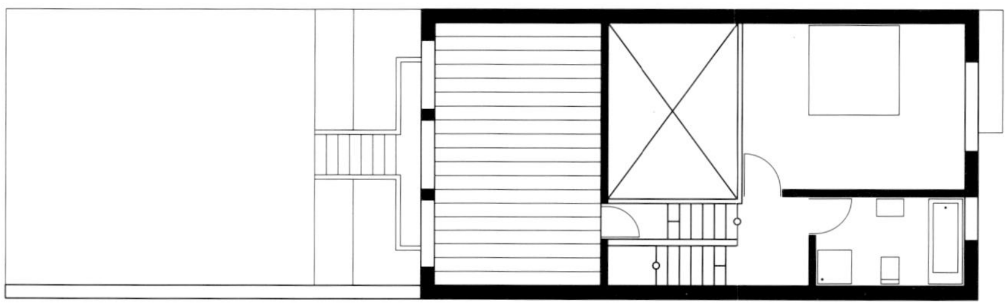

Upper floor

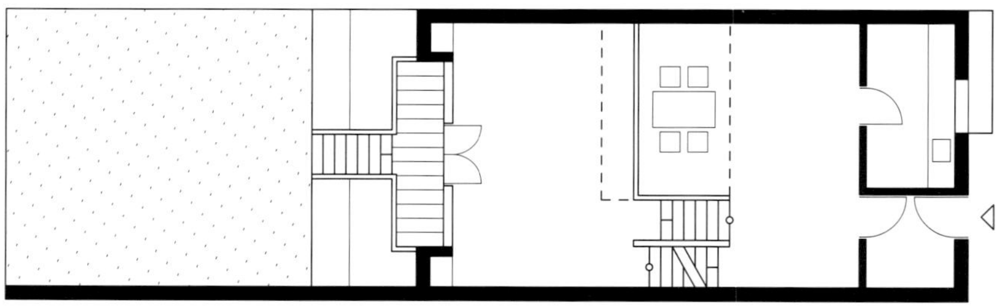

Ground floor

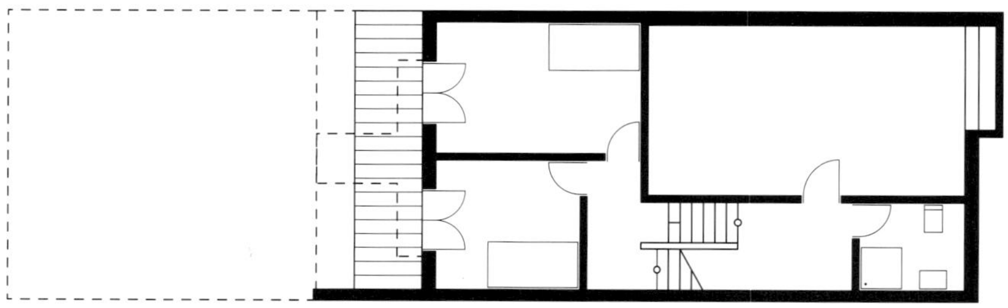

Basement

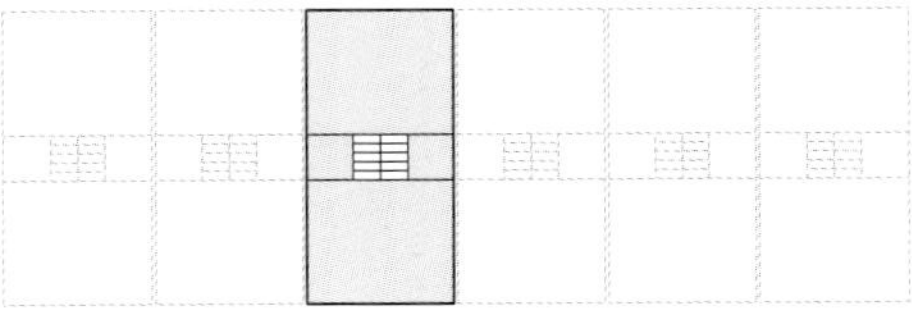

Longitudinal split-level
Three storeys
North-south orientation

This compact row house is situated in a rural environment; it features an extremely high floor-space index of 0.9. In addition to its compact exterior dimensions, the house's interior is organised very economically. The staircase with flights of equal length is placed in the middle of the house and directly adjacent to the party wall. This results in a classical split-level layout. Kitchen and dining area are located above the entrance level; the living room is half a level below. These two areas are spatially connected. The half staircase accommodates the different site levels so that the living room also opens up to the site. The personal rooms together with a bathroom are located on the split levels. The vertical circulation axis ends in a large roof terrace. The fact that the bathrooms do not receive natural light is a tribute to the economy of the floor plan; if one were located on the top floor daylighting would, of course, be possible.

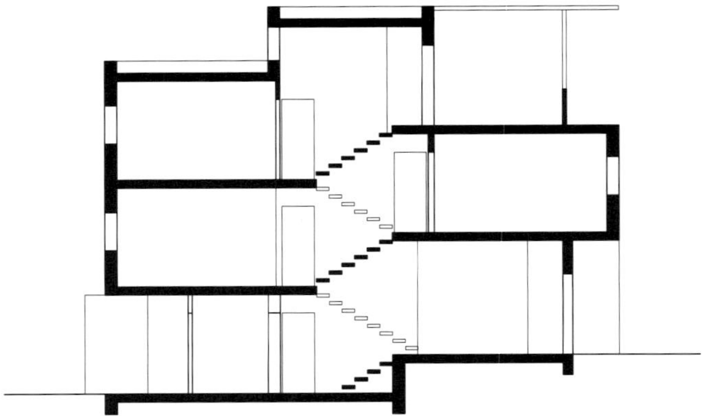

Cross section

2nd upper floor

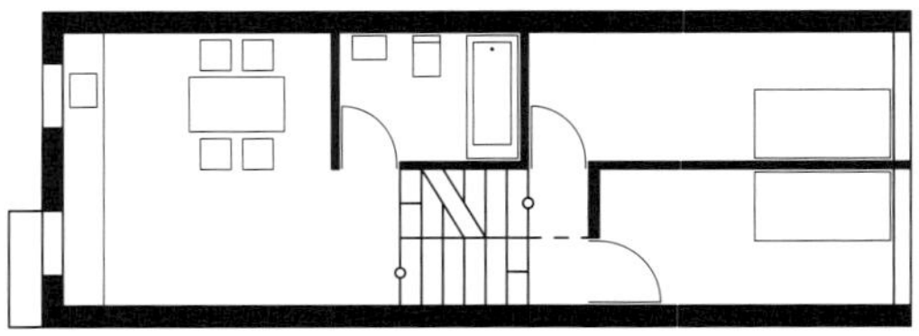

1st upper floor

Group of houses "Nofels"
Feldkirch, 1993
baumschlager & eberle

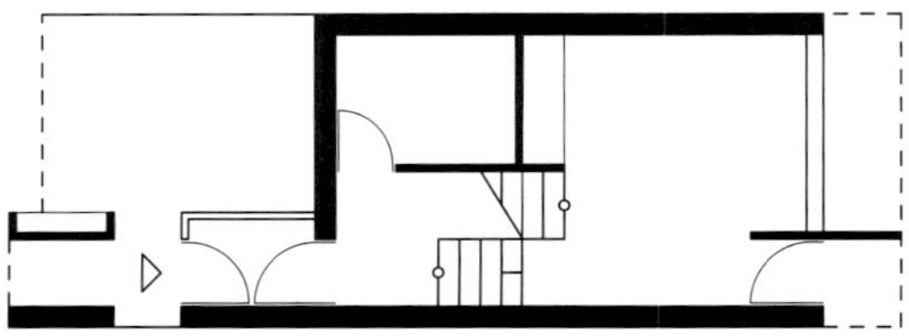

Ground floor

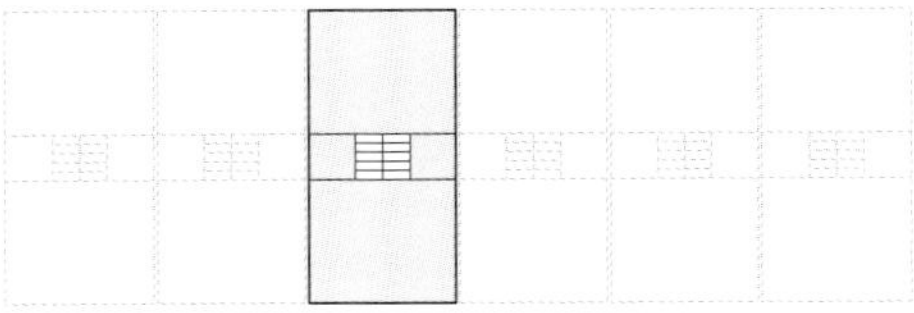

Longitudinal split-level
Three storeys
East-west orientation

The small row house with approximately 85 square metres living space features a fully glazed winter garden, which extends across all storeys and is utilised to gain energy. It serves as an open space to be used year round and as energy storage or thermal buffer. The large expanse of glazing lets the transition from the interior space to the garden appear seamless. Depending on the orientation of the house, the roof glazing collects sunlight and reflects it into the rooms via the bordering walls. This type comprises two axes. The north axis contains the eat-in-kitchen on the lower level and personal rooms on the upper levels. The south axis accommodates the staircase, the living rooms, utilities and the entrance area. The basic model can be extended in every direction, for example by adding another room axis on the other side of the staircase. Thus, a highly flexible and almost energy self-sufficient house typology could be created.

LBS "System houses" project
Freiburg, 1996
Günter Pfeifer

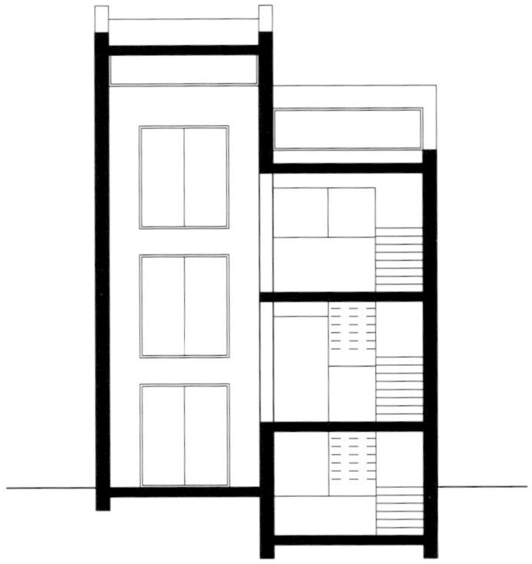

Cross section

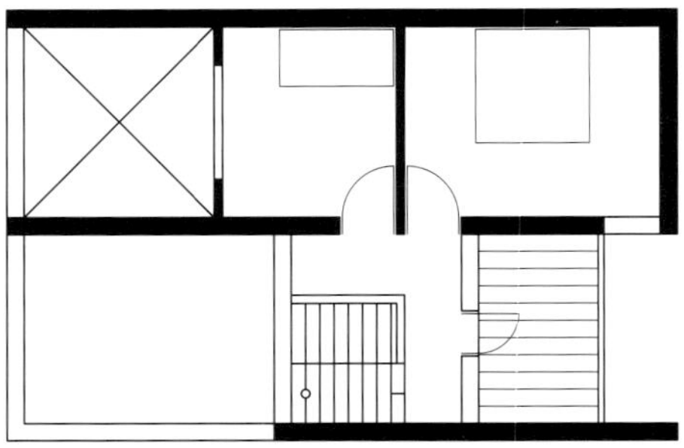

Top floor

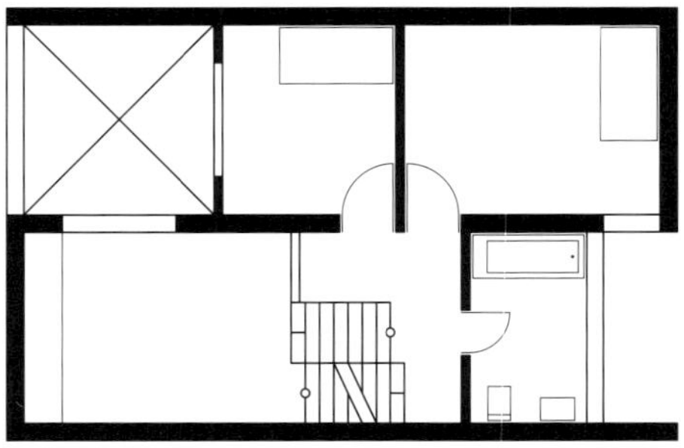

Upper floor

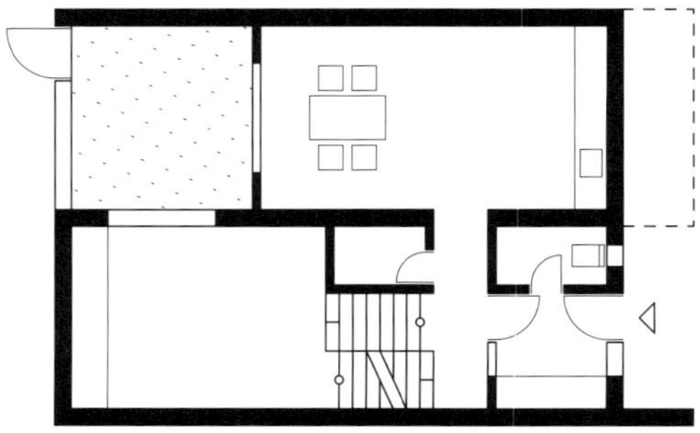

Ground floor

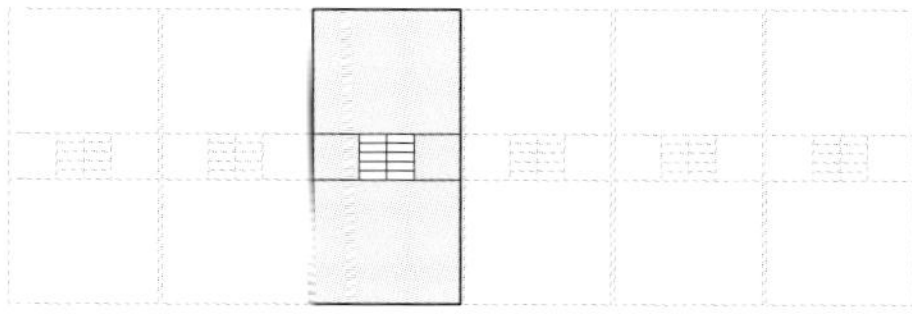

Longitudinal split-level
Three storeys
East-west orientation

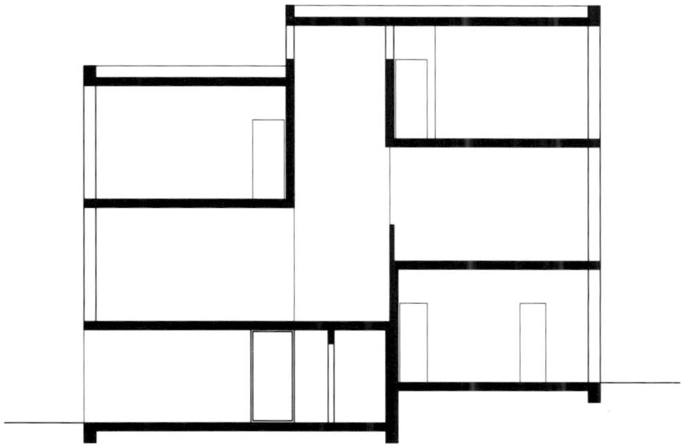

Longitudinal section

This classic split-level house type with a parking space integrated into the floor plan is compact and economical. Apart from the landing staircase, there are no other access areas such as hallways. A two-storey open space visually connects all levels and provides daylight for the dining area in the centre of the house. Except for the personal rooms, the landing areas are integrated into the rooms. The split-level arrangement and the intermediate open space give the rooms an intimate and self-contained character. This house type can easily be linked to an adjoining unit via the landings. Its simple structure and compact arrangement offer a particularly economical construction.
One deficit is the lack of exterior spaces. Only the use of partition walls can provide appropriate privacy. Extending the staircase would allow the realisation of a roof garden. The rear side of the house should not be exposed to local nuisance factors since this is where the personal rooms are to be found.

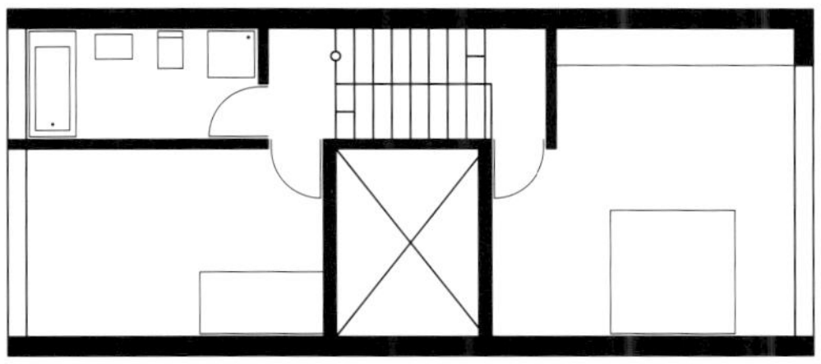

Top floor

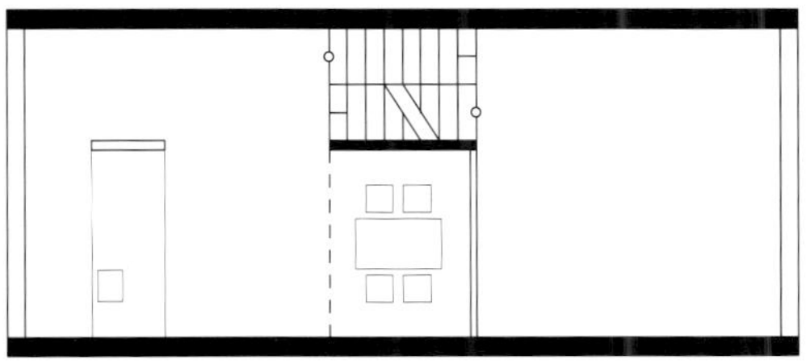

Upper floor

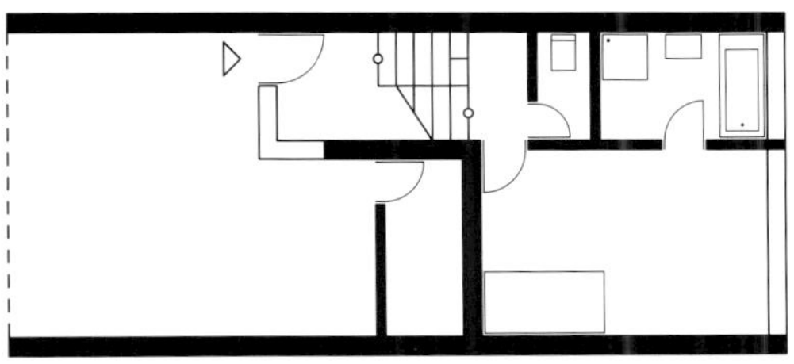

Ground floor

Student project
Darmstadt University
Sebastian Schaal

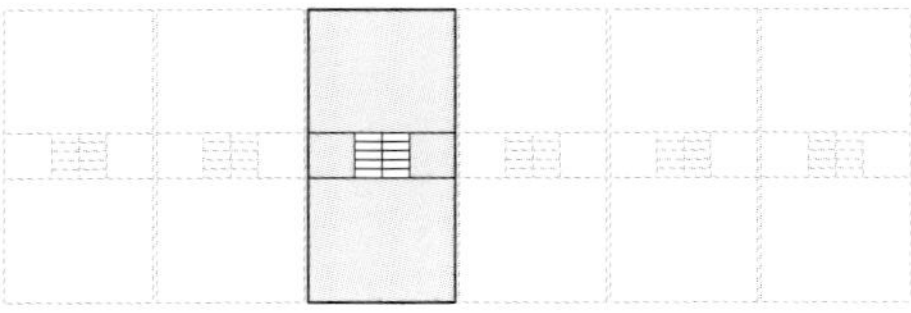

Longitudinal split-level
Three storeys
North-south orientation

An "energy garden" extending over 2.5 storeys forms the centre of this split-level house type which is divided into two vertical zones. Depending on the orientation of the house, it not only acts as a spatially connecting element, but can also be used to supply energy if it is covered with a transparent roof. The floor plan is divided into a narrow secondary room zone that also includes the access zone, and a zone for common and personal rooms. The dimensions of the latter can be adjusted to suit local conditions. Recesses in the façade create space for open areas that can be used as a parking space in front of the building or as a secluded terrace at the back.

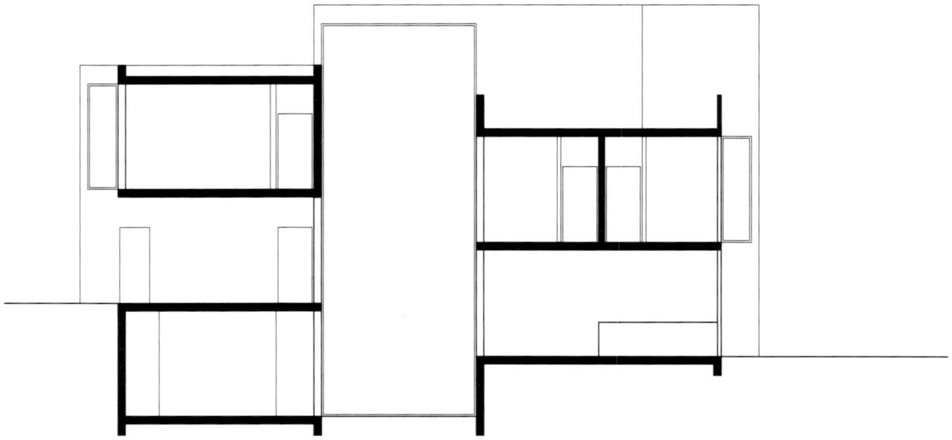

Longitudinal section

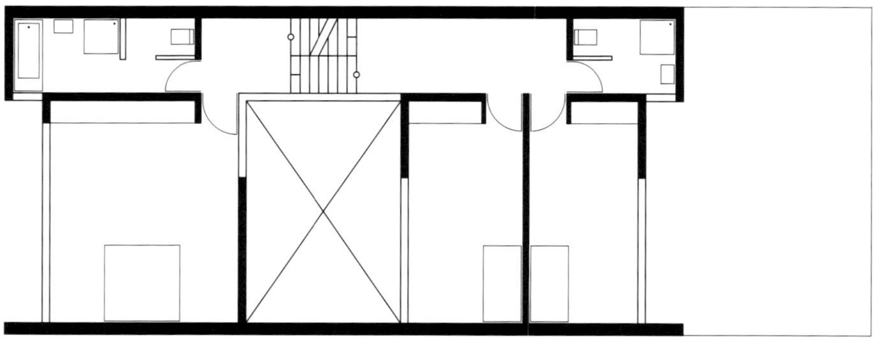

Upper floor

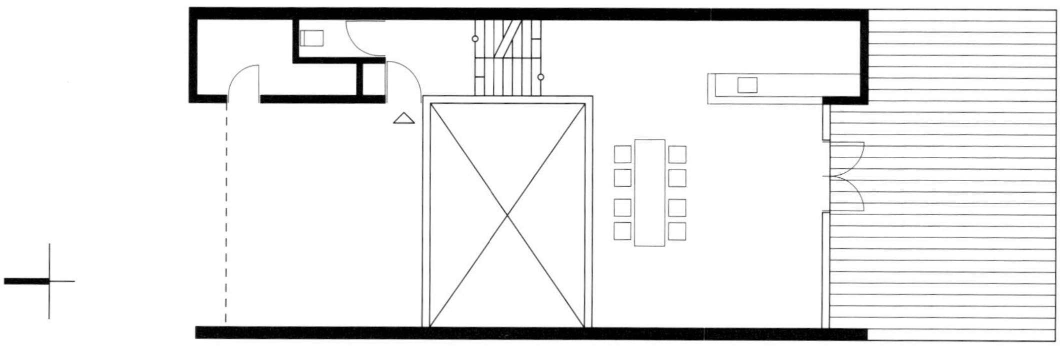

Ground floor

Student project
Darmstadt University
Martin Trefon

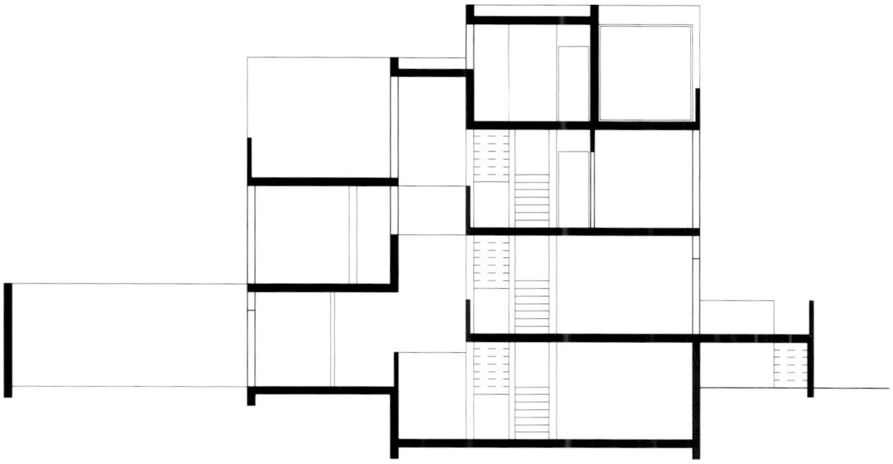

Longitudinal section

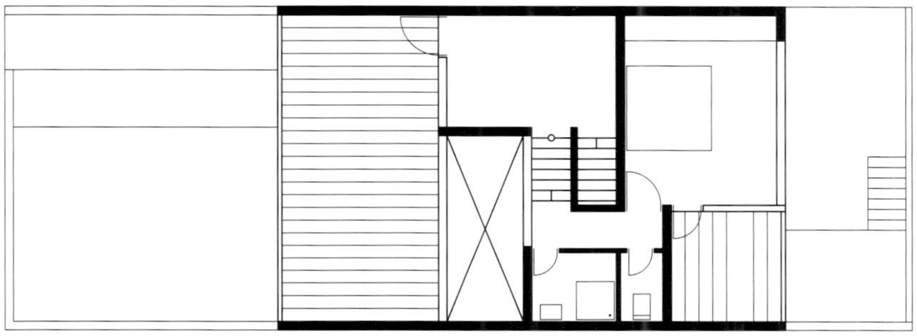

2nd upper floor

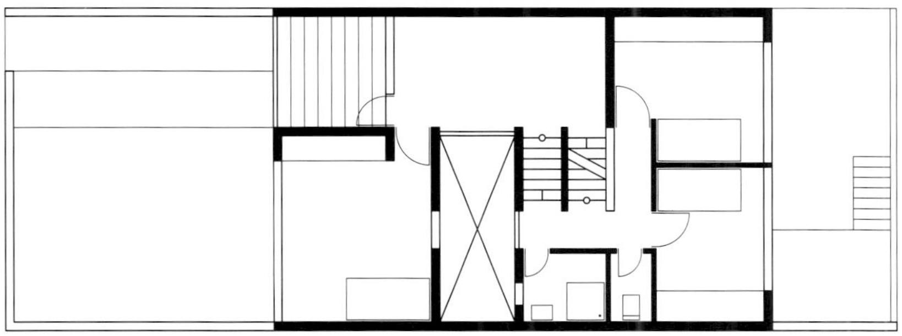

1st upper floor

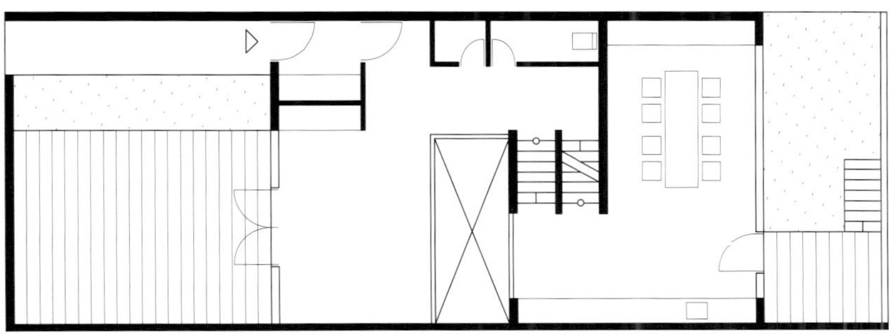

Ground floor

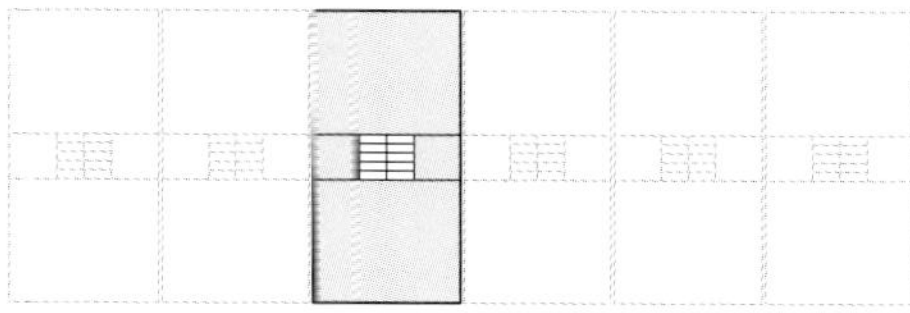

Longitudinal split-level
Four storeys
East-west orientation

This spacious house with a landing staircase arranged in cross direction offers multiple internal and external spatial interrelations. Despite the direction of the stairs, the split levels are separated lengthwise. This creates numerous daylighting options and several terraces on all levels. A three-storey open space in the centre of the house provides the deep floor plan with additional daylight and makes for selective internal visual connections. Featuring only four personal rooms plus additional spaces in the half-basement, this relatively large house is not economical in terms of creating living space, and it offers almost no options to use parts of the house independently. However, its strength lies in its spatial complexity and the captivating overlap of internal and external spaces.

Student project
Darmstadt University
Catrin Kuchta Schrader

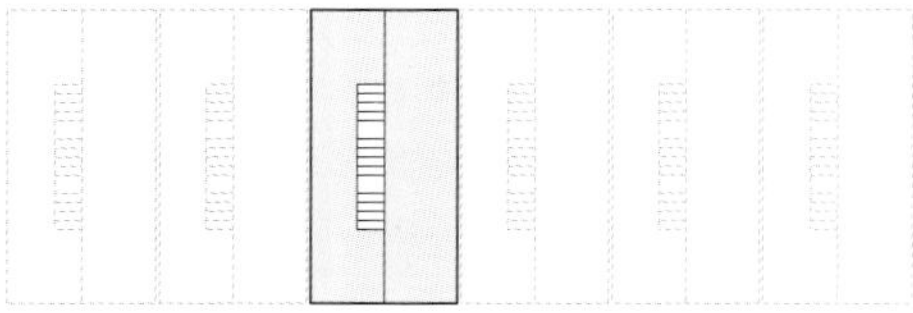

Transversal split-level
Two storeys
East-west orientation

This house type was developed in 1967. Its split-level structure, arranged across the width of the building, is particularly economical and makes for a diversified spatial experience. It is also very flexible in terms of individual user concepts and different family sizes. The floor plan is developed around two fixed cores: the staircase with entrance and toilet, and the kitchen with a bathroom above. Two staggered split-levels span the space in between; they can be used in different ways. A skylight provides the inner zone with daylight via a central light shaft. From the staircase, a catwalk leads to a secluded roof terrace. Based on the open layout of the floor plan, this house type features a high degree of spatial interlocking in a very small space. The spaces adjacent to windows can be separated by walls or divided with wardrobes.

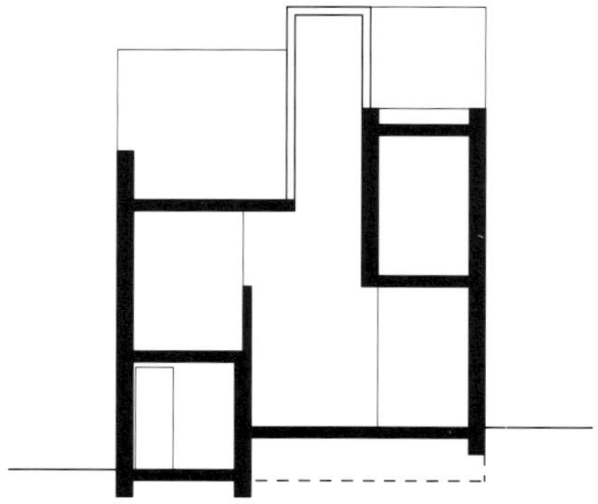

Cross section

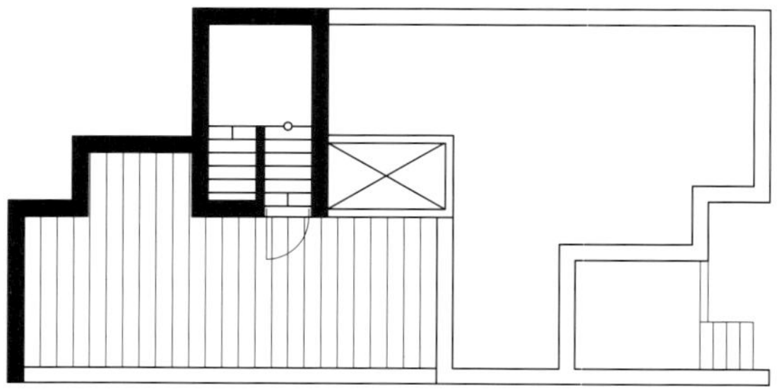

2nd upper floor

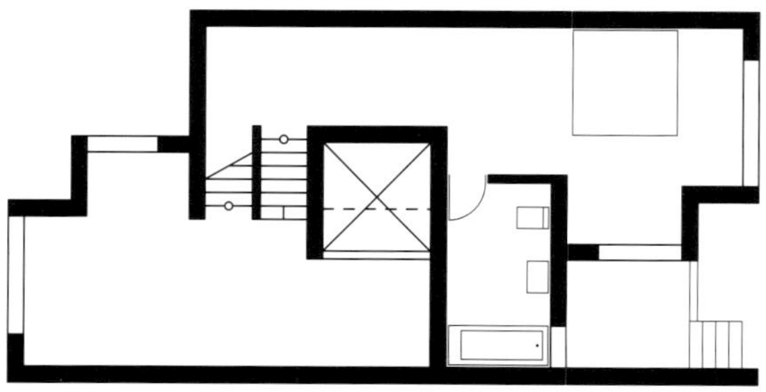

1st upper floor

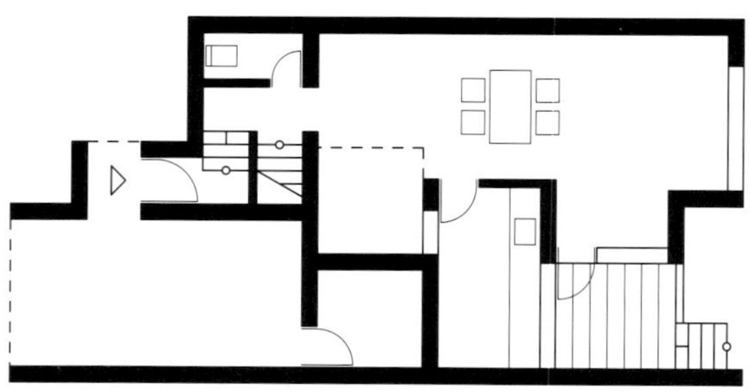

Ground floor

"Diagoon Houses"
Delft, 1971
Herman Hertzberger

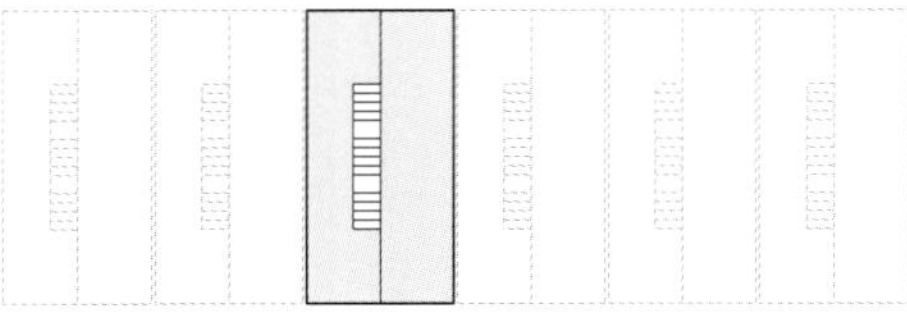

Transversal split-level
Two storeys
North-south orientation

This small house type with just two personal rooms is particularly economical and at the same time creates complex spatial interrelations. The resulting high-quality space is complemented by an arrangement of different exterior spaces such as a balcony, a loggia and a garden courtyard. A horizontal organisation into two zones is typologically characteristic for this house type, as is the split-level arrangement. A narrow building axis comprises a two-storey open space above the entrance area, bathrooms and a small room. The broader building axis with another open space above the living area allows natural south light to reach deep into the space. A larger personal room lies above the living area with its south-facing terrace oriented towards the garden courtyard. It features a window facing the open space above the living area. This house type can be extended to comprise further storeys and/or can be linked to the adjoining unit via the staircase landing.

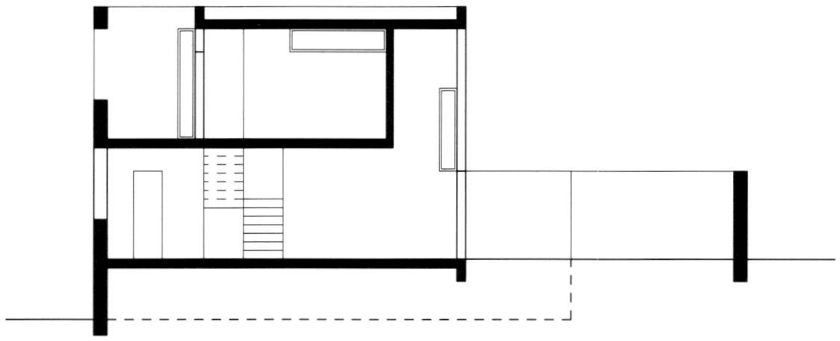

Longitudinal section

Top view of the roof

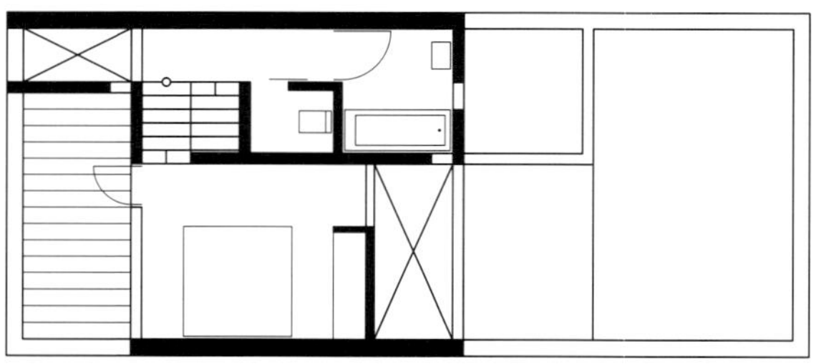

Upper floor

Student project
Darmstadt University
Per Brauneck

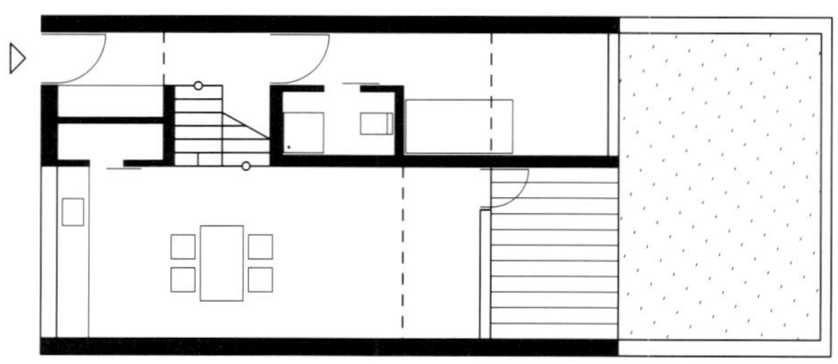

Ground floor

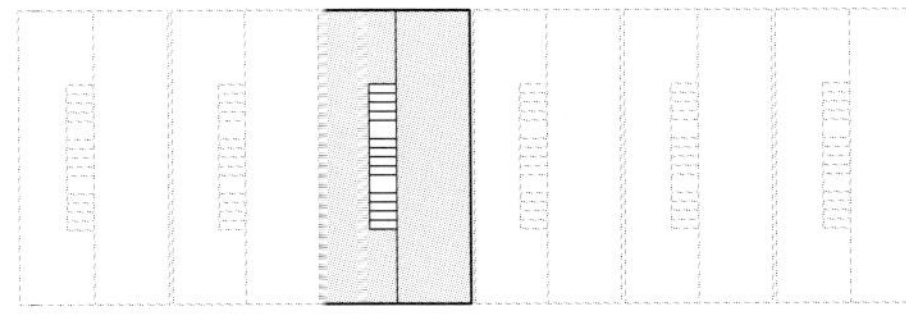

Transversal split-level
Three storeys
East-west orientation

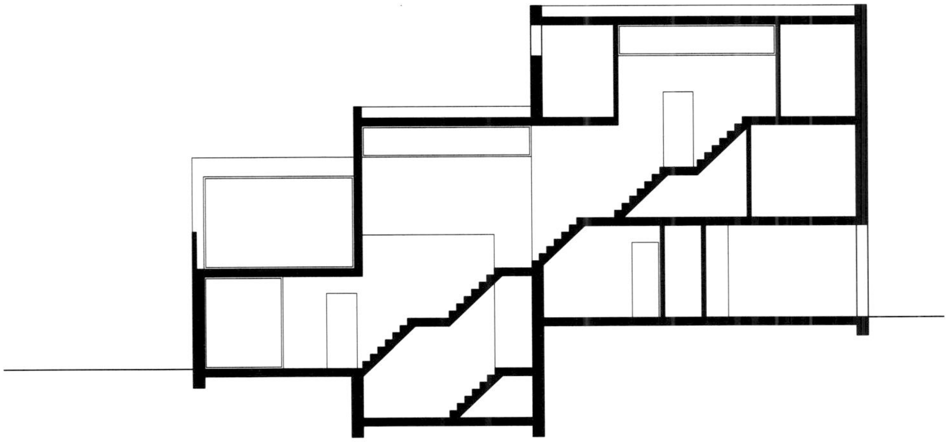

Longitudinal section

This house type is a split-level variant with a continuous central staircase with rooms arranged on both sides of it. The rather unconventional positioning of the stairs results in an exciting spatial arrangement. The staggered building volume allows for extensive daylighting from all sides and includes the possibility of exterior spaces on almost all levels. The common zones are distributed over different levels in the centre section of the house and are linked with each other via open spaces and across the split-levels. Personal rooms are located on the upper levels and feature their own bathroom. The room next to the entrance can be used independently, if desired. The staircase leads to a small loggia that could be developed into a roof terrace. Due to the elongated staircase including various landings, this house type can accommodate topographical conditions particularly well. It does not provide options to link to neighbouring units.

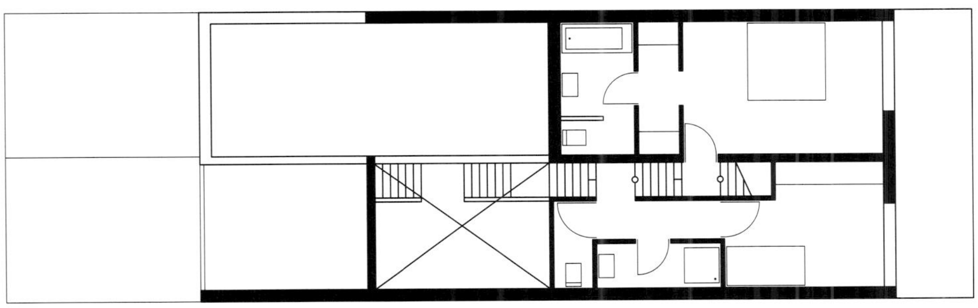

1st upper floor

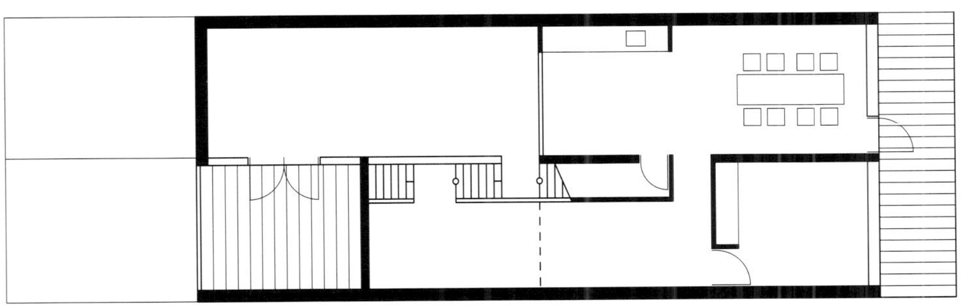

Ground floor

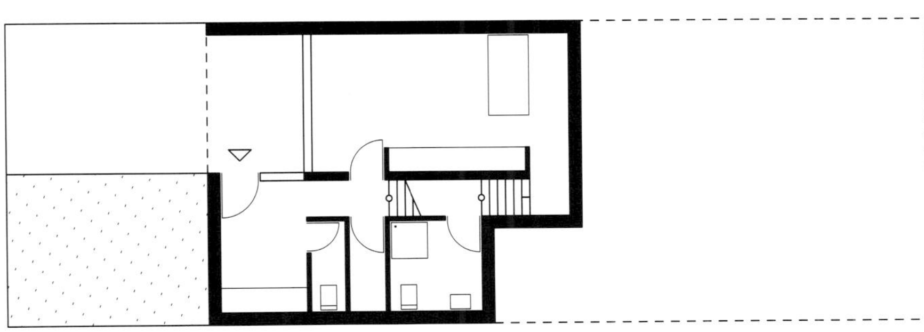

Basement

Student project
Darmstadt University
Felix Mantel

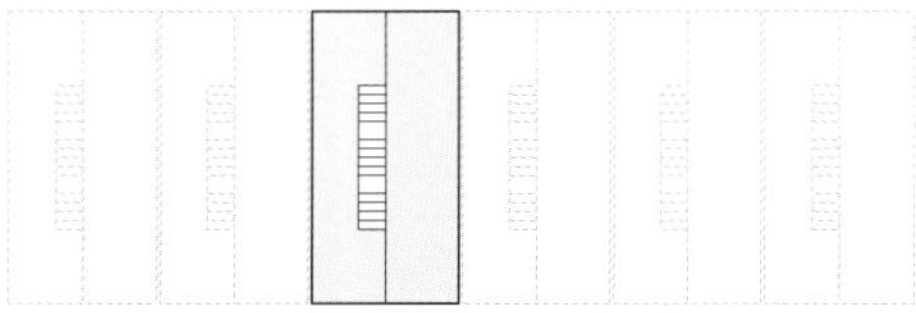

Transversal split-level
Three storeys
East-west orientation

The house type with continuous, centrally located staircase requires the storeys to be staggered along the longitudinal axis of the house. This principle leads to dynamic spatial overlaps, visual relationships and cross connections. Immediately upon entering the house, the long staircase as characteristic feature provides a view of the entire spectrum of rooms. An eat-in-kitchen is located on the entrance level with direct visual connection to the living room area, which lies half a storey deeper. Narrow personal rooms are staggered above, each accessed from the staircase landing. As these three rooms, each with their own bathroom, are separated by air spaces, they give the impression of great discreteness. The last room alongside the long, single-run staircase is a large bedroom, also equipped with its own sanitary facility. The furnishing concept offers an intelligent solution to overcome the disadvantage of the narrowness of the room. The end of the staircase axis leads to a small balcony.

Student project
Darmstadt University
Martin Trefon

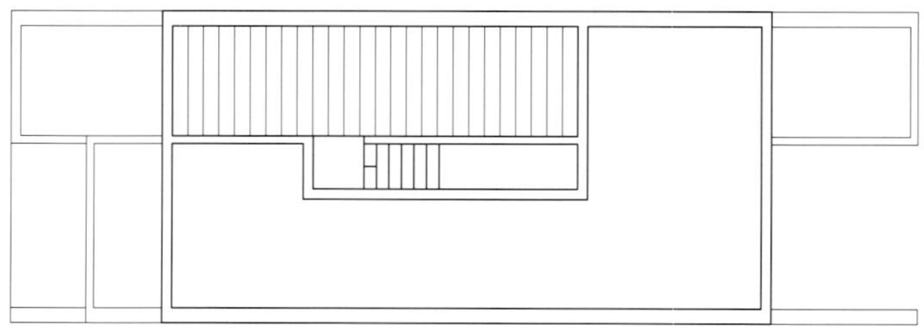

Top floor

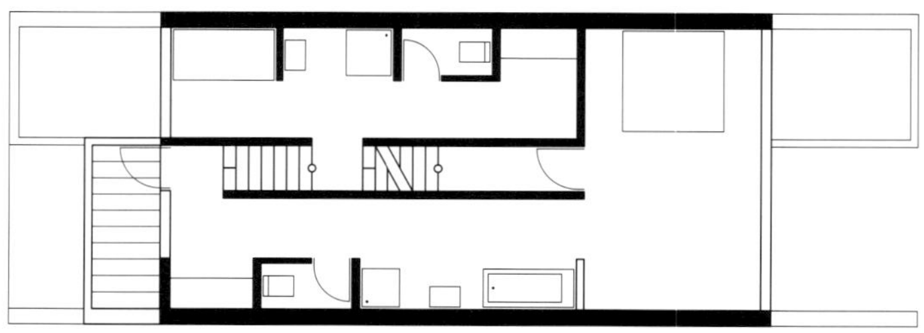

2nd upper floor

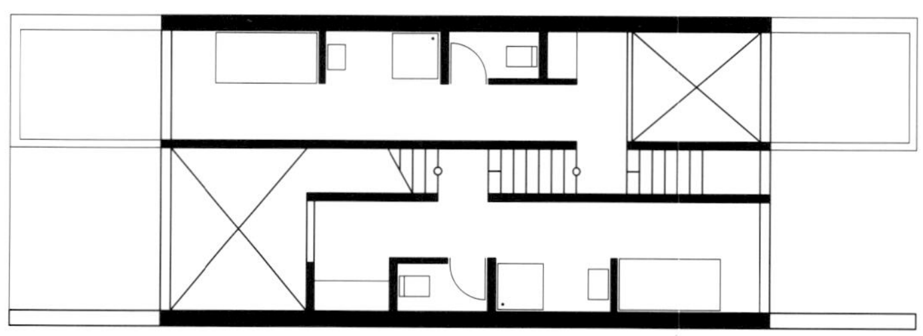

1st upper floor

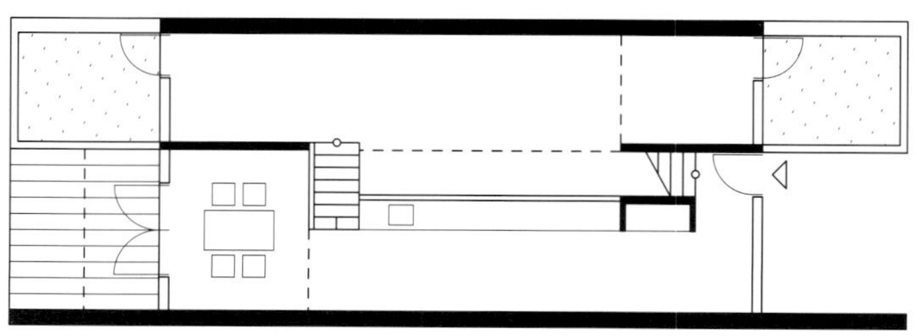

Ground floor

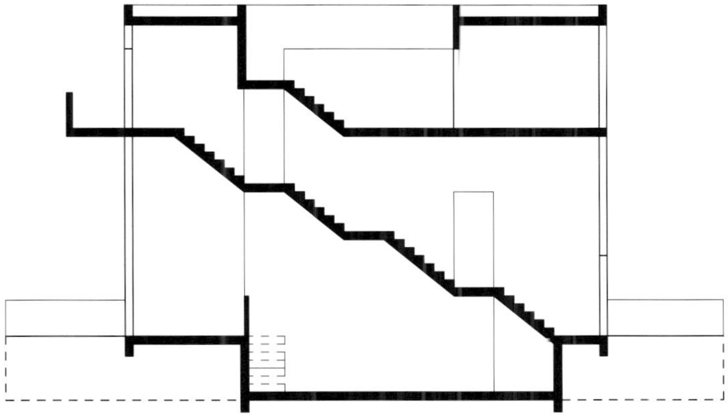

Longitudinal section

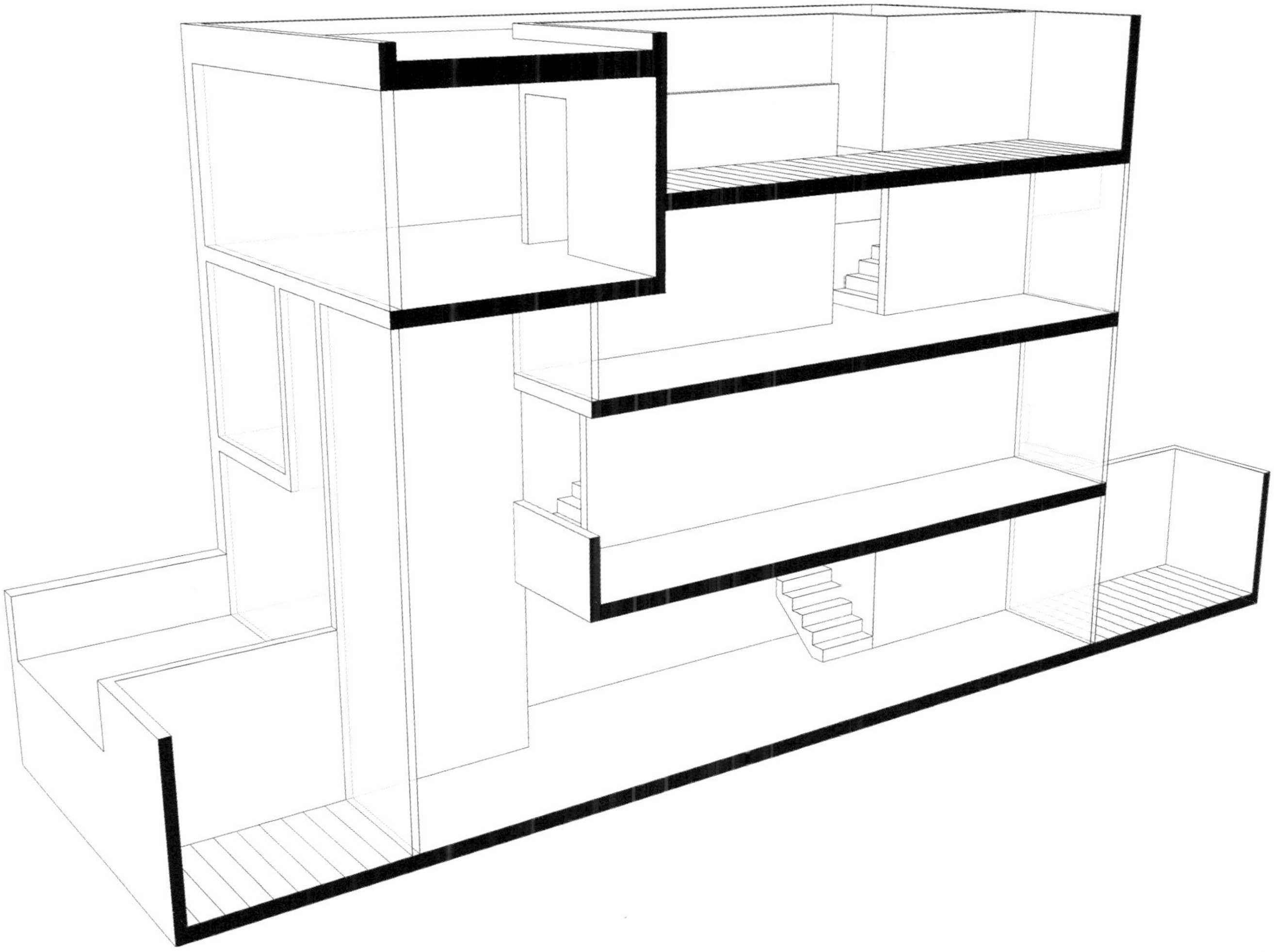

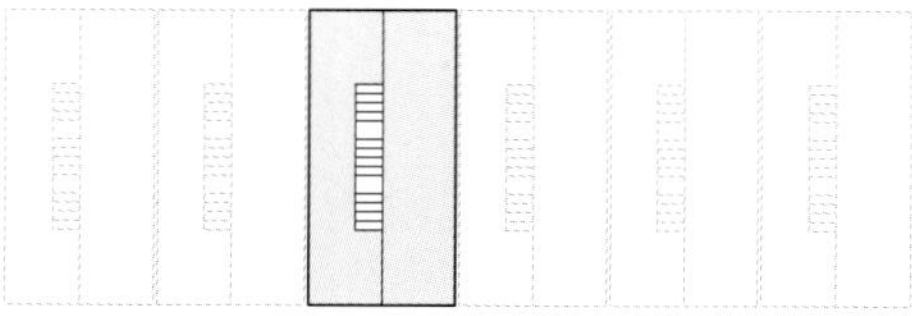

Transversal split-level
Three storeys
North-south orientation

This row house type combines the patterns of a split-level and a duplex apartment. The floor plan is divided into a zone with separate rooms to the north and a common zone facing south. A large loggia integrated into the south façade separates the dining from the living area and can be developed into an "energy garden". The personal rooms are located half a level up or down from the living area. The number of rooms allocated to a flat is flexible and can be easily adjusted via the length of the hallway; also structurally, more individual rooms can be realised easily. The ground floor could also be used commercially. The height of this house type can even be expanded to create a multi-storey apartment unit. Since the access zone lies on one side of the house, an adjoining unit could be accessed from it without further structural work. This house type can also be arranged in an east-west orientation.

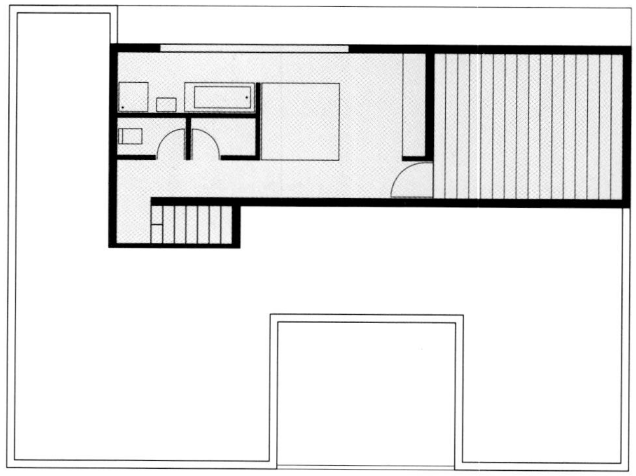

Top floor

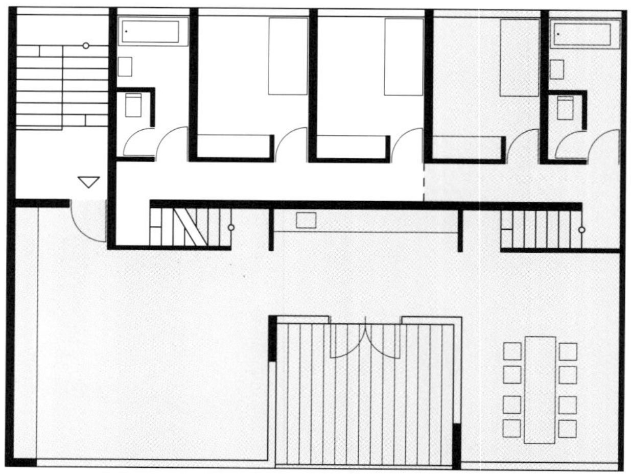

Upper floor

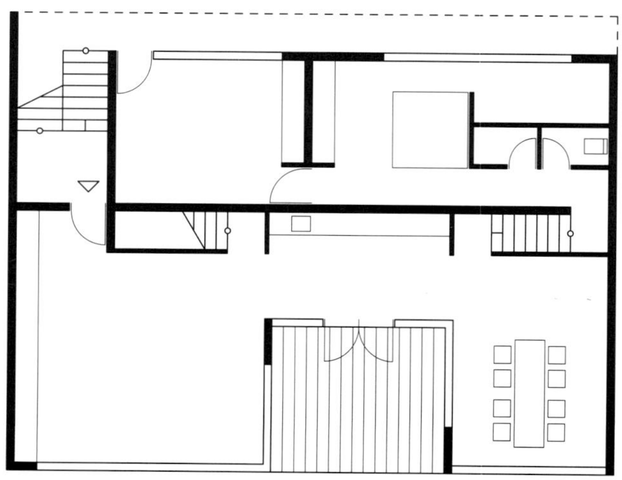

Ground floor

Student project
Darmstadt University
Jörn Rabach

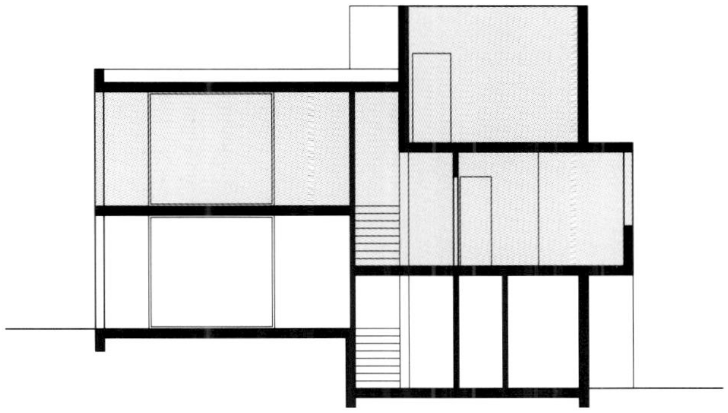

Longitudinal section

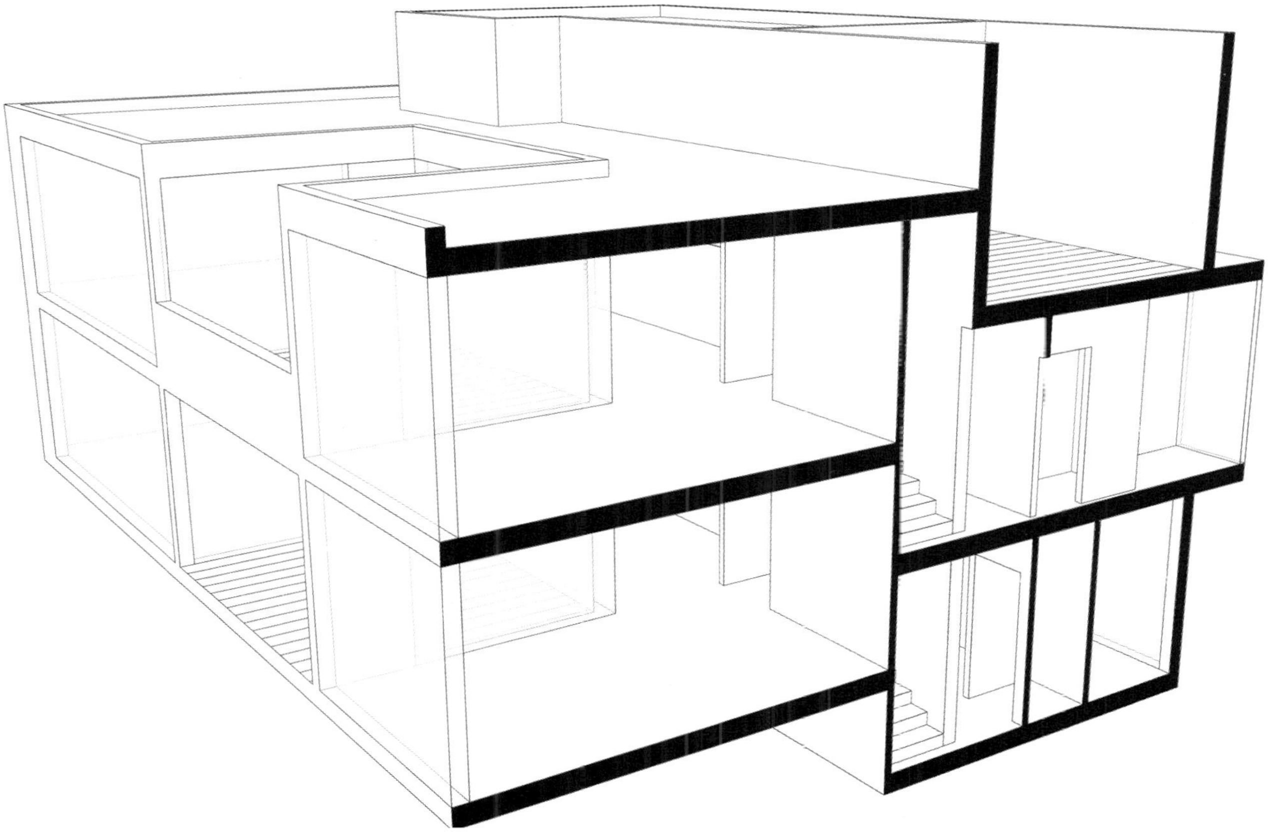

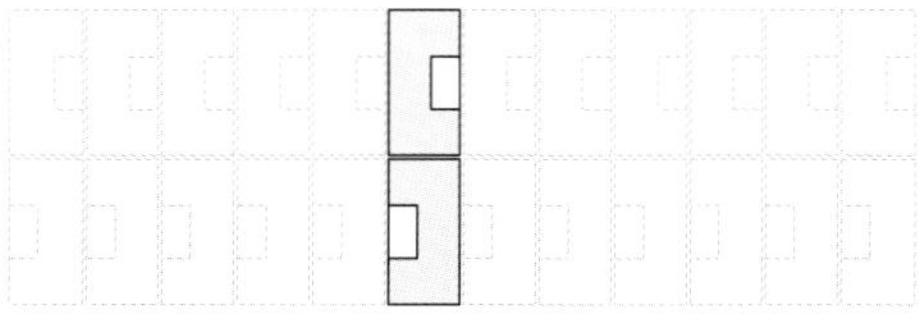

Back-to-back
Two storeys
North-south orientation

This introverted housing development in Carmona comprises 16 small back-to-back row houses that receive daylight through an inner courtyard. The rear end of the house, which is attached to the neighbouring house, is offset – as can be seen in the sectional drawing – resulting in row houses that are interlocked with each other. This arrangement can be further developed into an extremely dense urban structure and can adjust to varying topographic levels.

The houses comprise a living and dining room on the ground floor that is directly adjacent to the inner courtyard. This courtyard can be used as a secluded open space year round. On the street side, in front of the kitchen and the entrance, is another courtyard that can serve as a storage facility. The first floor comprises three small personal rooms and a bathroom.

The location of the staircase provides the opportunity to connect different units with each other. The design of this house type is adapted to its location by its orientation.

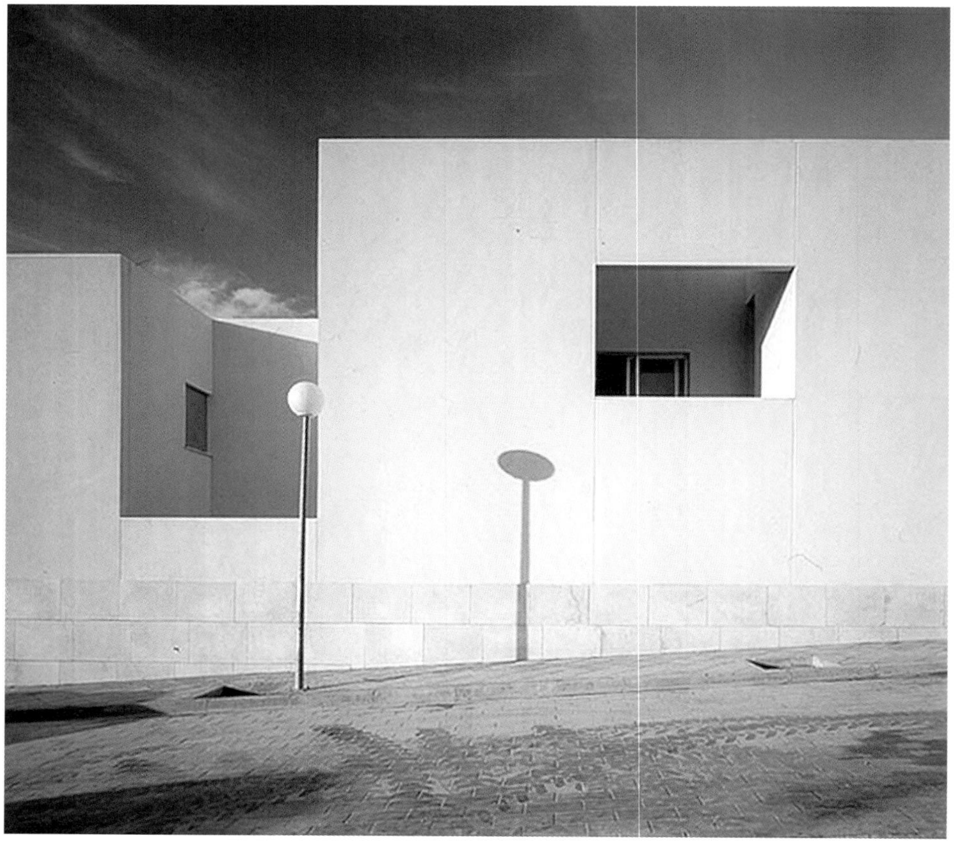

Residential complex
Carmona, 2003
Oscar Gil Delgado

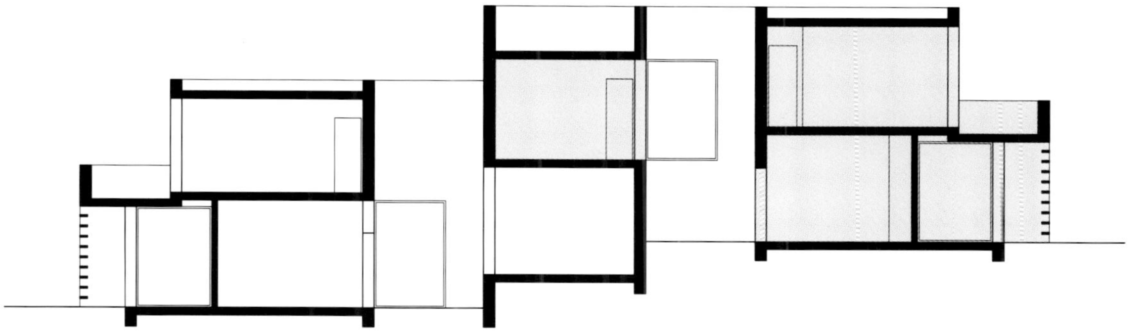

Longitudinal section

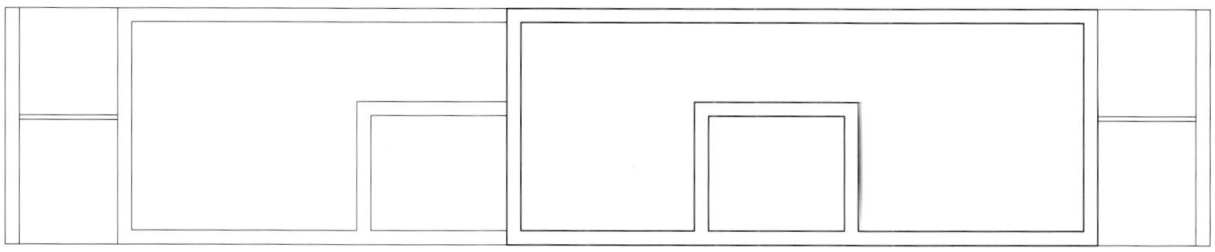

Top view of the roof

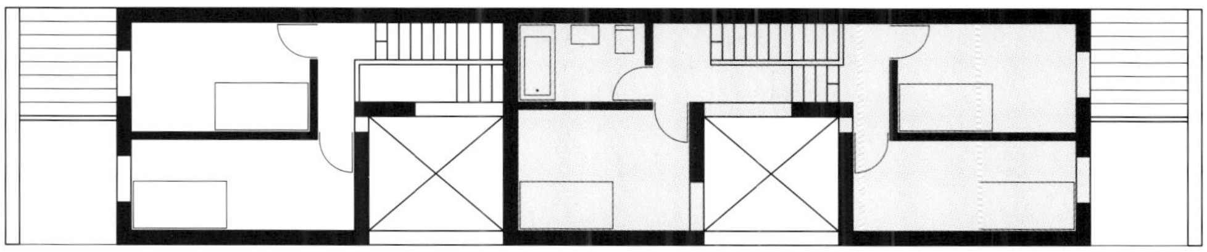

Upper floor

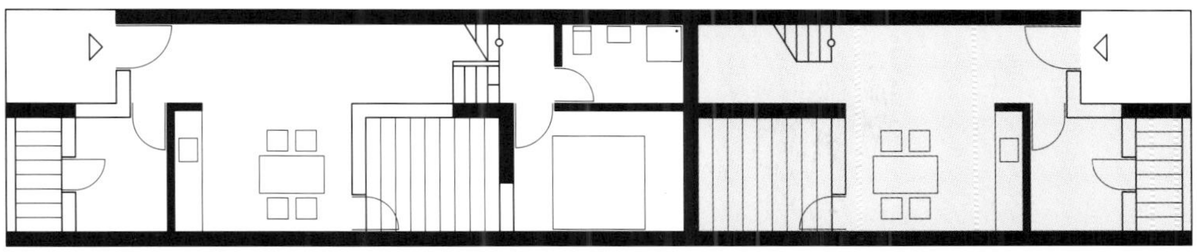

Ground floor

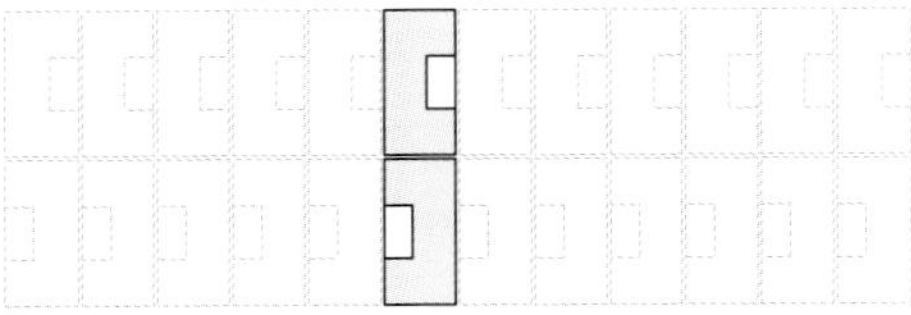

Back-to-back
Two storeys
East-west orientation

This two-storey, back-to-back structure consists of modules comprising three different apartment units each. Two flats with an upper floor lie back-to-back to a single-storey flat. This single-storey unit is based on a one-sided orientation, whereas the two-storey units with a large roof terrace on the top floor feature double-sided orientation. Overall, this structure is characterised by a highly economical use of space. The floor plans of the flats include almost no hallways: the personal rooms of the single-storey unit are accessed via a central living room, and those of the two-storey flats via the staircase landing. Bathrooms are combined in a central zone running the length of the building and do not receive natural light. Within the modular group, floor plans cannot be modified. However, modifications are possible in terms of the urban development structure that can create high-quality exterior spaces despite the high density of the layout.

Ringstraße development
Neu-Ulm, 1999
Fink + Jocher

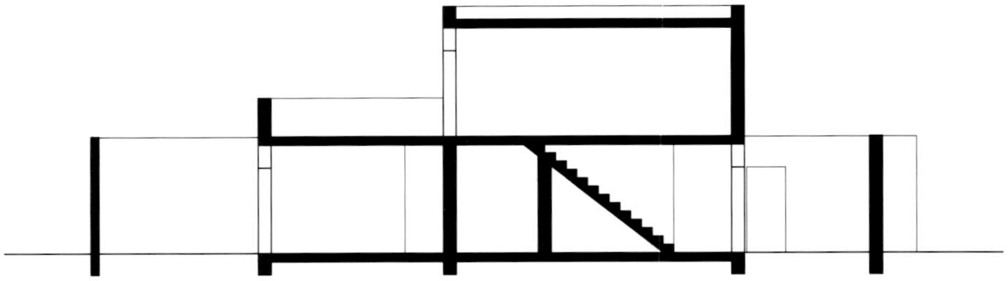

Longitudinal section

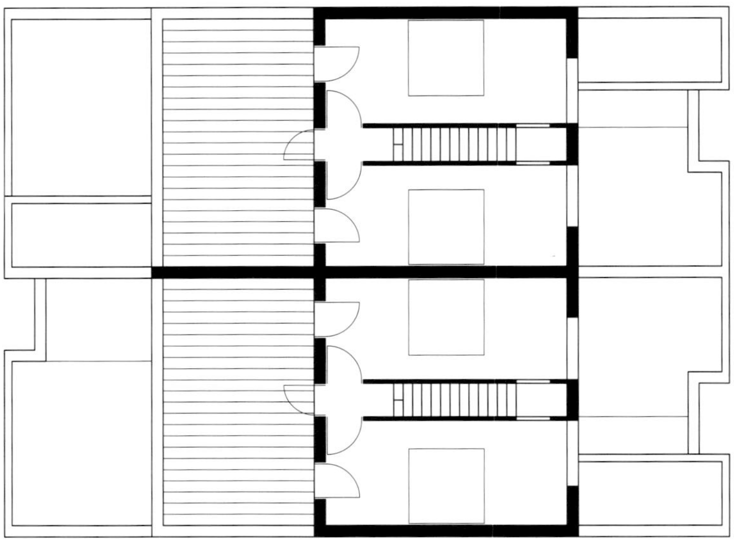

Upper floor

Ground floor

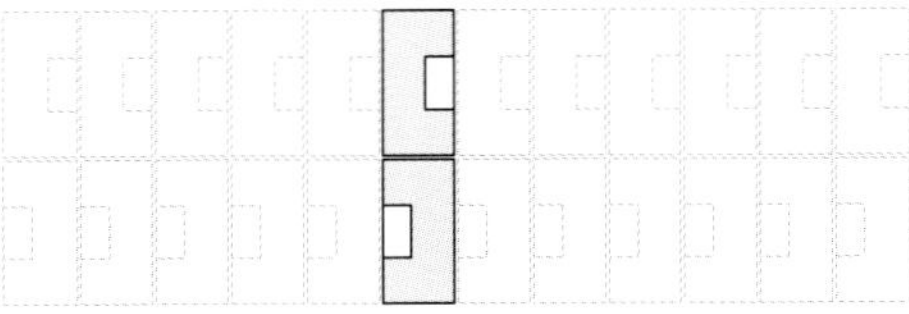

Back-to-back
Two storeys
East-west orientation

These two-storey, back-to-back row houses feature a south-facing courtyard. A single-flight landing staircase leads from the living space on the ground floor to the inner courtyard located roughly half a storey higher. The staircase also connects the living space to two personal rooms on the first floor via a mezzanine. The result is an exciting arrangement of spaces on a minimal footprint. An open area between the bathroom and the smaller personal room can be used as a play or work area. Alternatively, an additional open space in this location could further enhance the complex interlocking of spaces, and a third level with a roof garden and an additional personal room could be added. Furthermore, the layout of the circulation permits linking opposite houses, which would result in apartment units of different sizes and a lively overall arrangement.

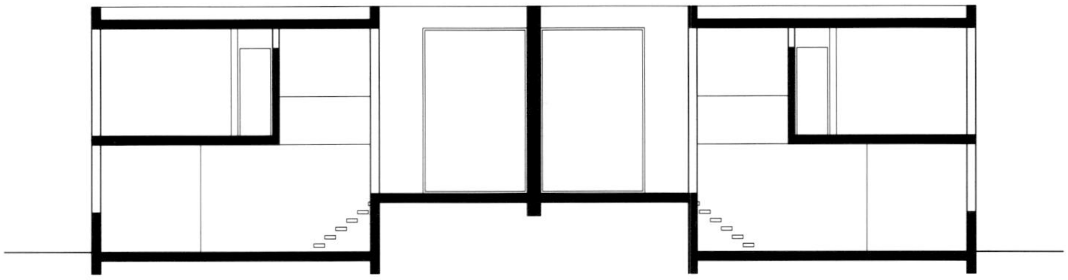

Longitudinal section

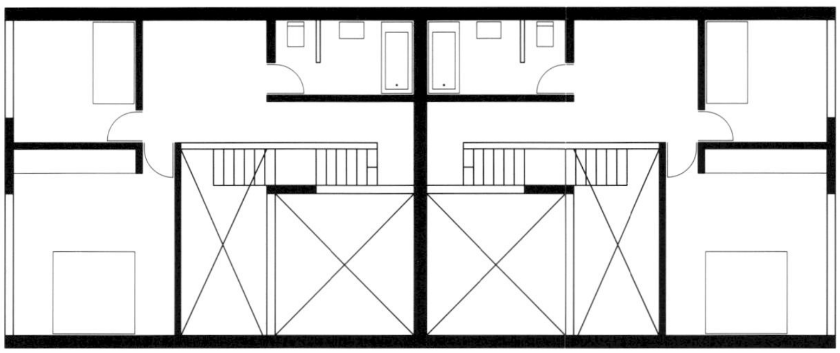

Upper floor

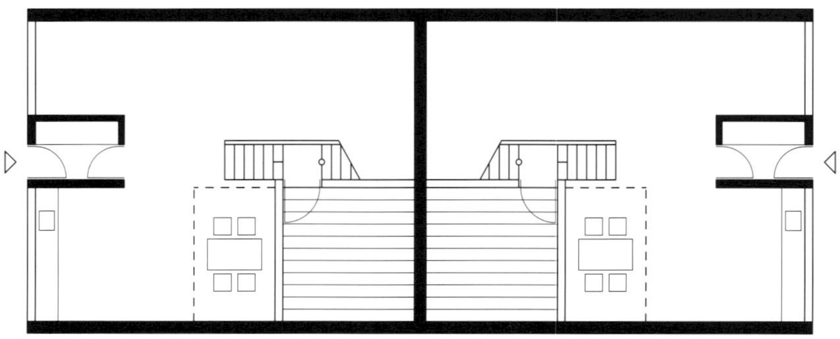

Ground floor

Student project
Darmstadt University
Kai Dibutch

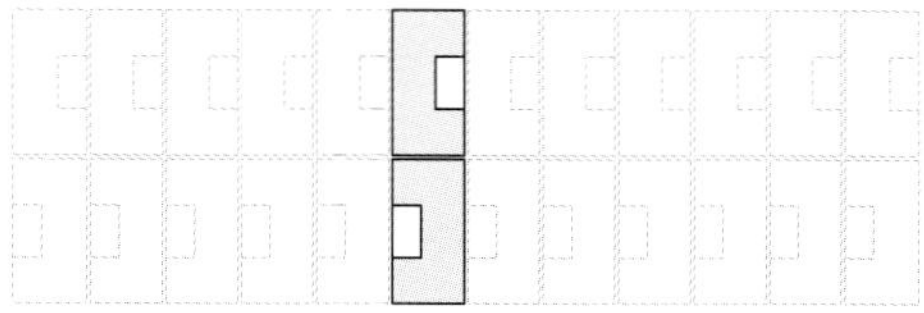

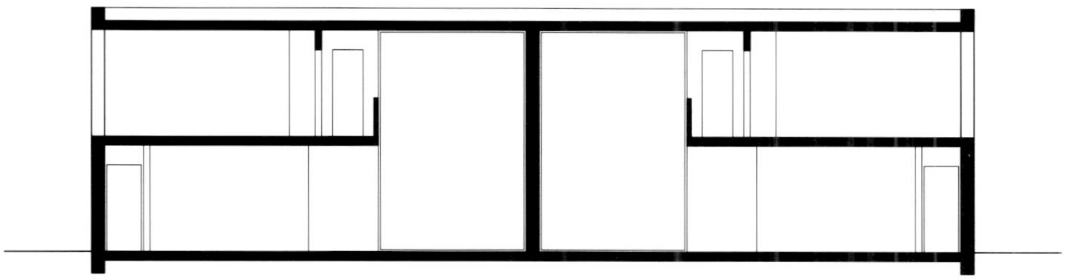

Longitudinal section

Back-to-back
Two storeys
East-west orientation

The typological characteristic of this back-to-back row house with east-west orientation is the offset of the apartment units across one room axis, shown in the sectional drawing. Thus, one personal room of one unit lies above the living space of the neighbouring unit. This shift causes the staircase, which on the ground floor lies on the side of the house, to shift to the centre of the floor plan on the first floor, resulting in practically no hallway on the upper level. By inserting small hallways with doors, several room axes can be linked meaning that virtually any number of personal rooms can be adjoined to a living area. In addition, by using connecting doors on the ground floor, several living areas can be connected with each other. The structural flexibility makes this house type with its two-storey inner courtyard and the double-height garden room adaptable to social changes or to different requirements caused by changing stages of life. However, it does not offer privacy towards neighbouring units on the ground floor.

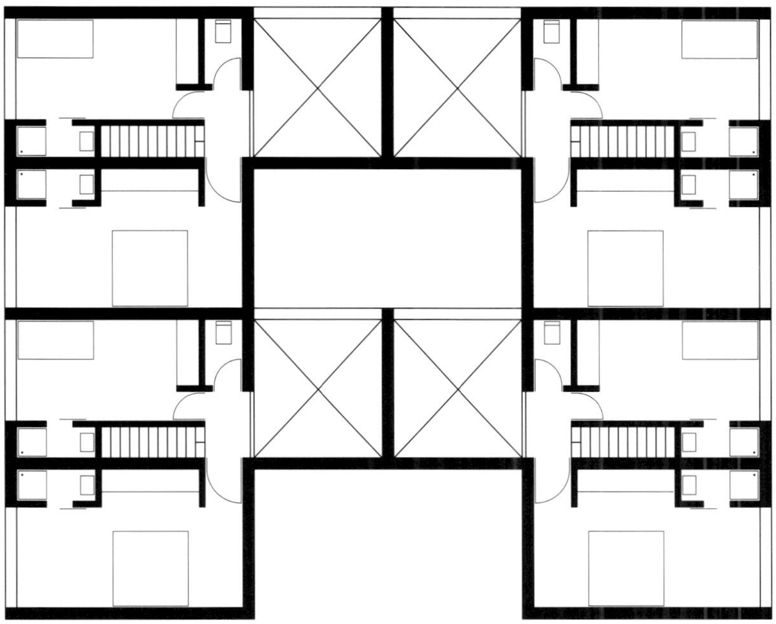

Upper floor

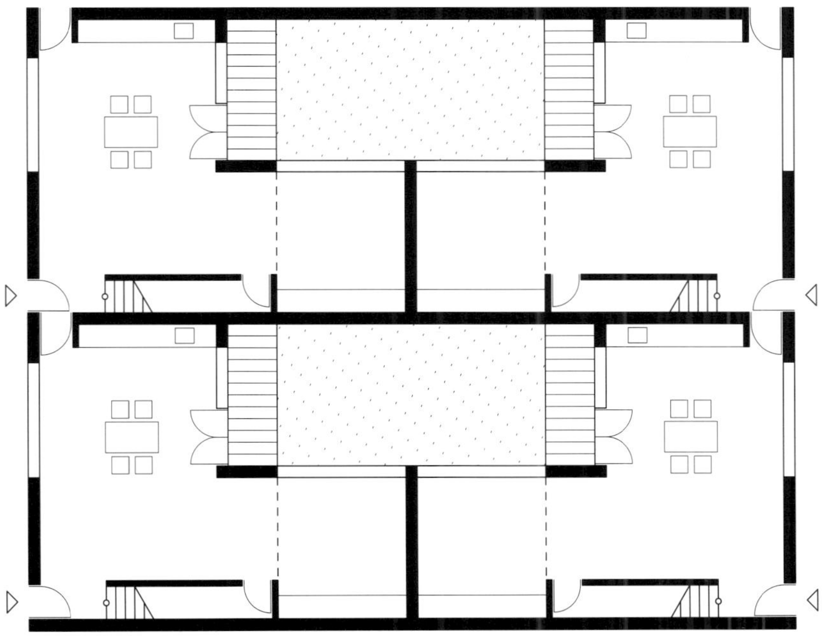

Ground floor

Student project
Darmstadt University
Sabine Svrcina

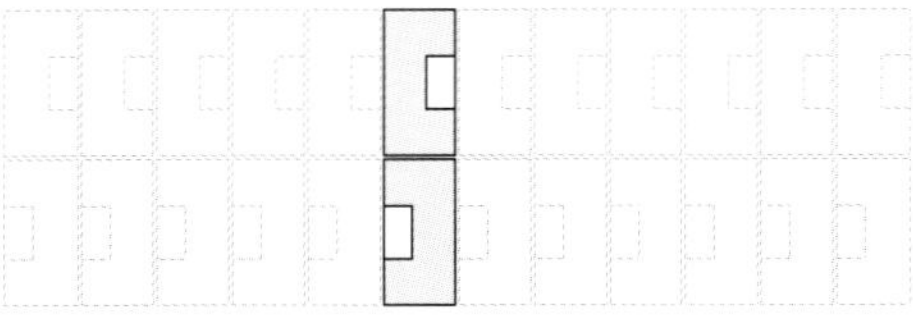

Back-to-back
Two storeys
East-west orientation

This two-storey back-to-back structure consists of six different units with four different apartment types. There are two duplex flats, each with two or three personal rooms per level, and four single-storey flats with two personal rooms each. All units are accessed via their own exterior entrance. Different apartment units can be linked within the structure. Each unit comprises two inner courtyards so that almost every room receives daylight from two sides. Mono-functional access areas in the form of hallways are kept to a minimum. Access zones are for the most part integrated into the rooms, creating a generous spatial arrangement. Varying views into and through the fully glazed courtyards forming integral parts of the floor plan enhance this impression. In addition to the courtyards, there are access yards in front of the entrances of the flats that form a transitional zone to the public street space.

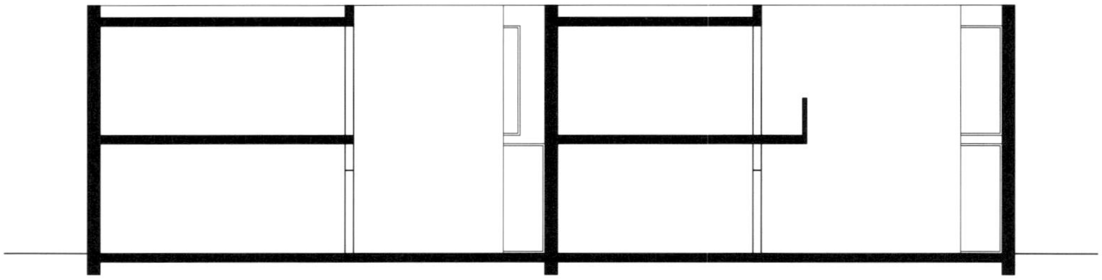

Cross section

Student project
Darmstadt University
Kai Dreker

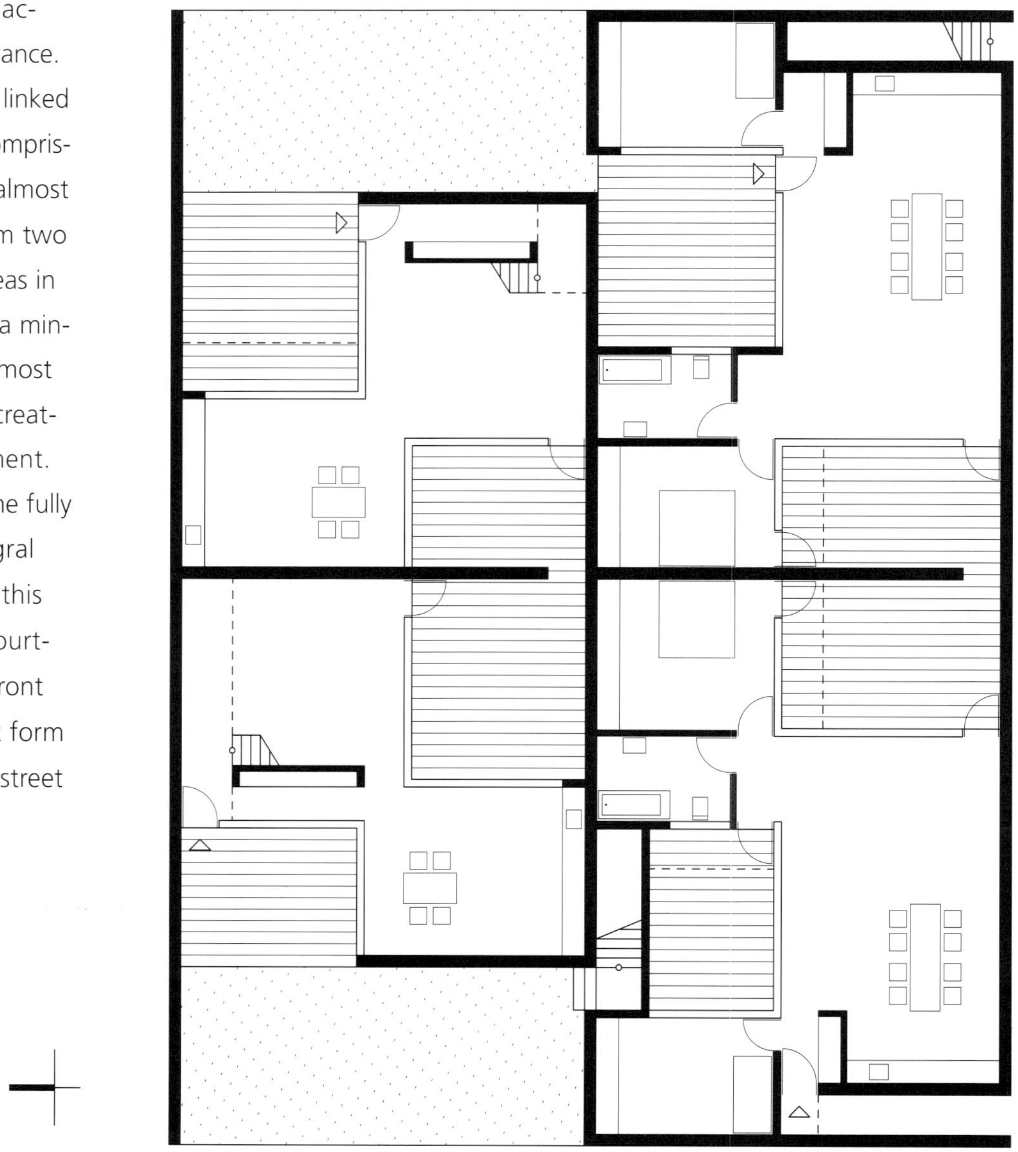

Ground floor

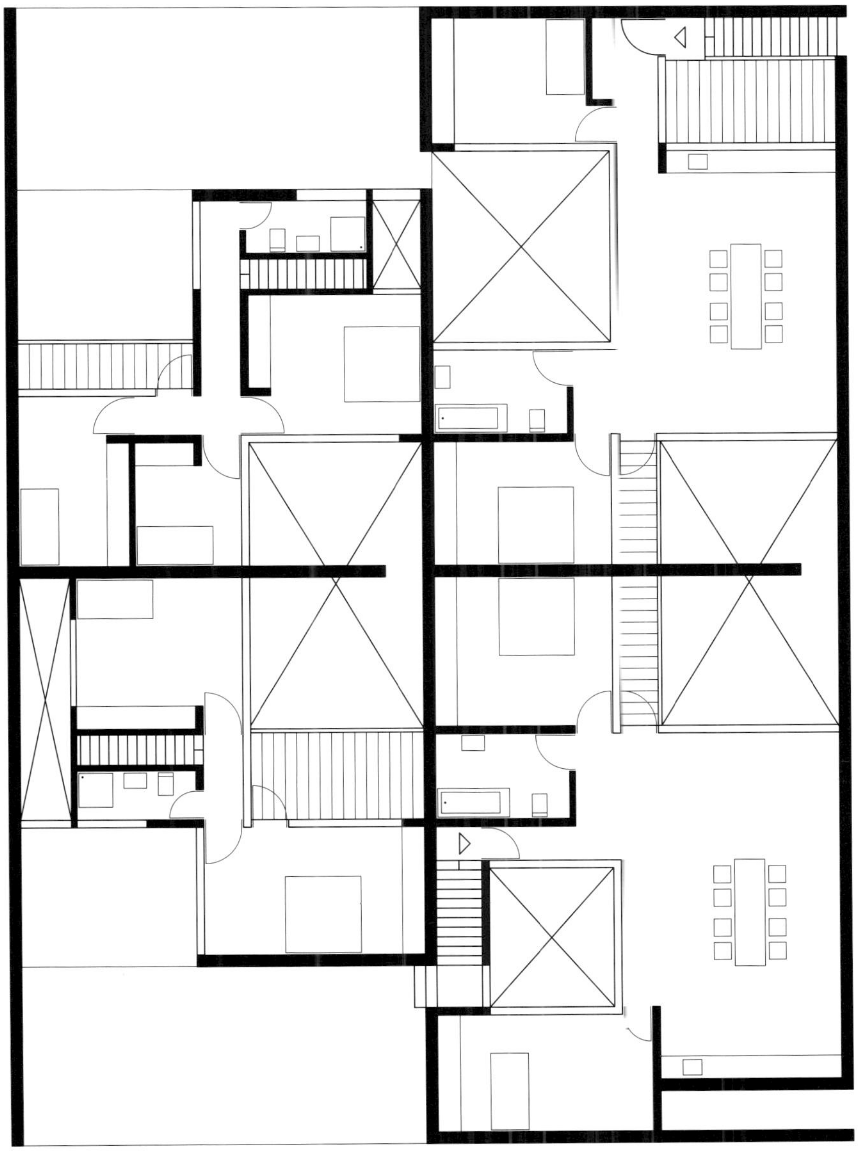

Upper floor

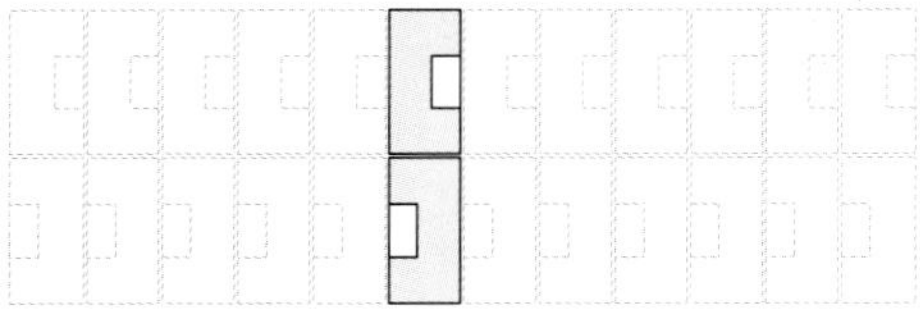

Back-to-back
Two storeys
East-west orientation

The structure of a residential development based on this house type is determined by small narrow alleyways on the ground level. By widening the alleyways within the entire complex, parking lots, green spaces and inner courtyards could be created that provide the development with a distinctive urban character. The house type itself is characterised by a tri-partition with an inner courtyard in the centre. The relatively wide floor plan with a continuous functional zone to the south accommodating all service rooms receives daylight exclusively via the two-storey inner courtyard. Small loggias on the first floor supplement the daylighting of the house. By changing the proportions of the courtyard, the width of the house as well as its length can be modified. Since the house receives daylight via the courtyard from all directions, it can have any orientation. The amount of light reaching a certain area can be controlled by the proportions of the courtyard. The house can be attached to adjoining units on the side comprising the functional zone.

Student project
Darmstadt University
Roland Pier

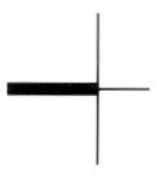

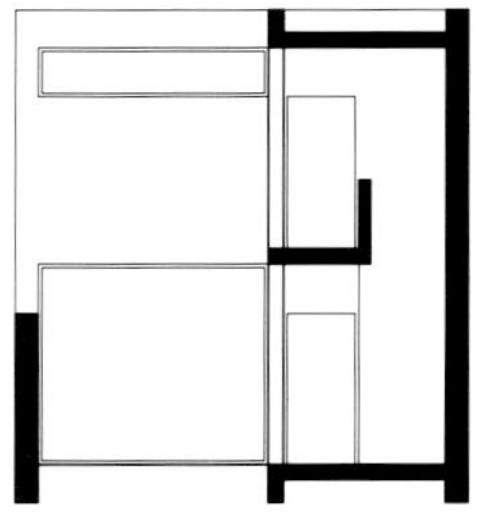

Cross section

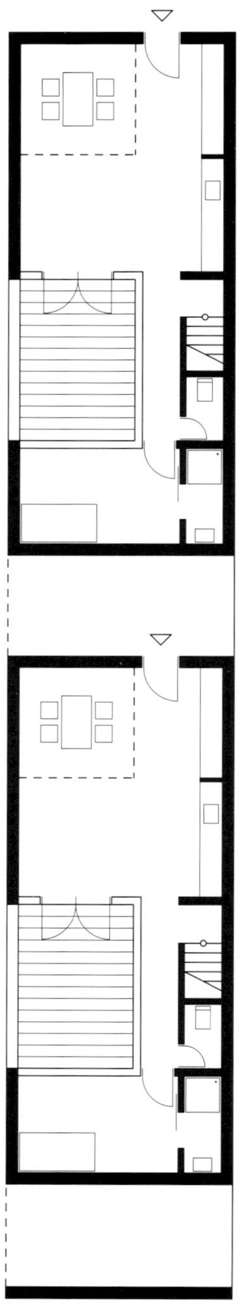

Ground floor

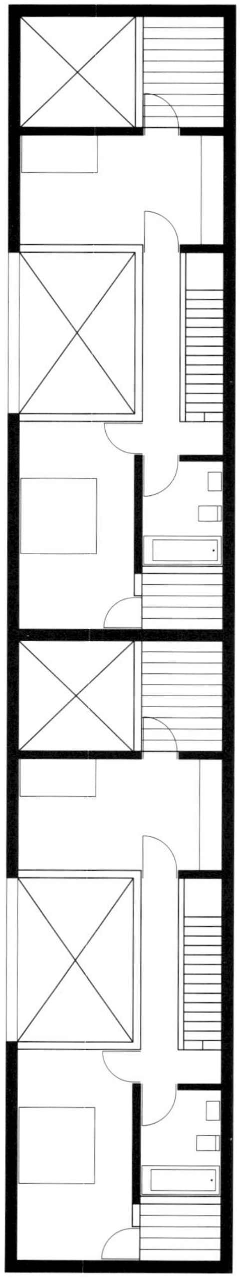

Upper floor

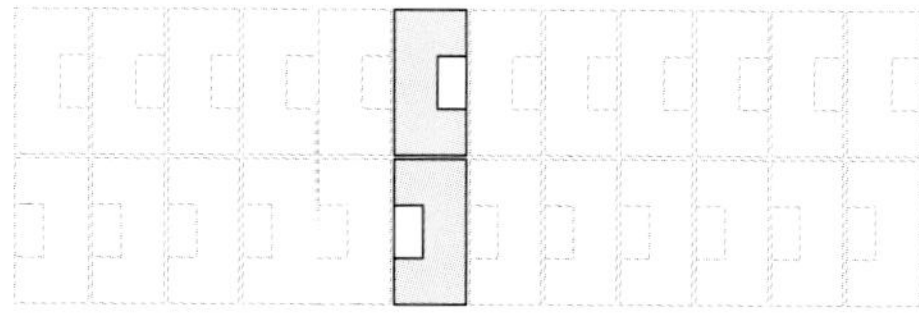

Back-to-back
Three storeys
East-west orientation

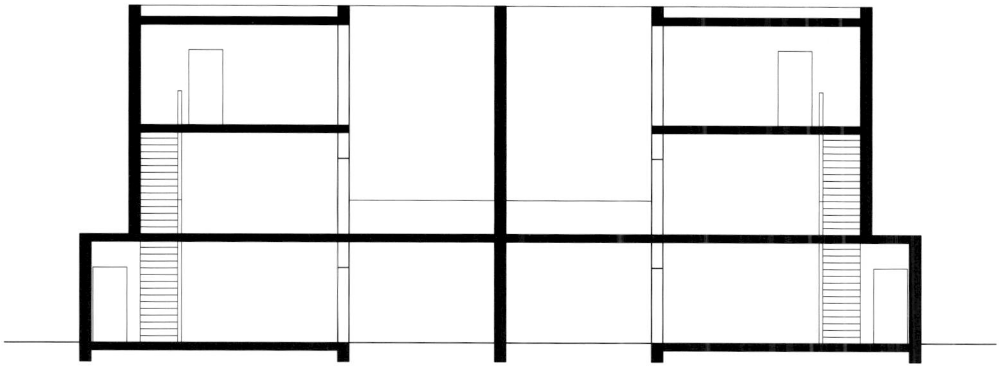

Longitudinal section

This narrow back-to-back row house type is characterised by its one-sided orientation with the access area on the north side and the living and personal rooms facing south. The spaces in this house can be allocated for certain uses at the resident's discretion; the example shown comprises personal rooms on the ground floor that could be rented out separately. The living room with kitchen, dining area and a terrace are to be found on the first floor. The second floor features two more personal rooms, each with associated bathrooms. The three storeys are connected by a single-flight stair. Whereas the width of the house is directly related to the length of the staircase, its depth is restricted by how far the sunlight can reach into the building. The three-storey courtyard – lit from the south - is particularly shady on the ground floor level. A modification of this house type with a deeper floor plan could include additional open spaces, which would provide visual connections between the rooms as well as additional daylight.

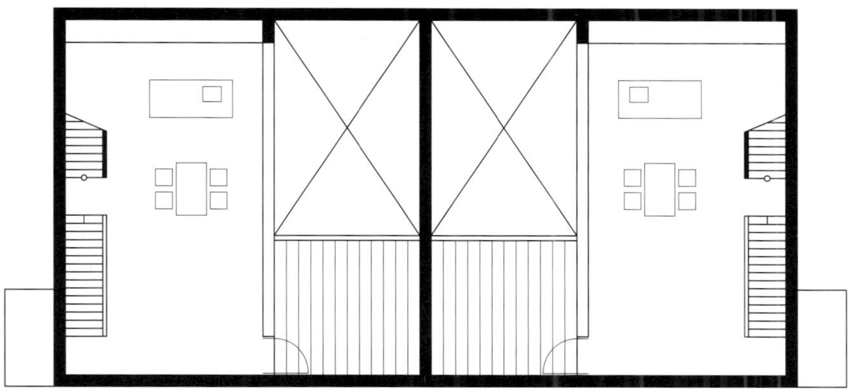

1st upper floor

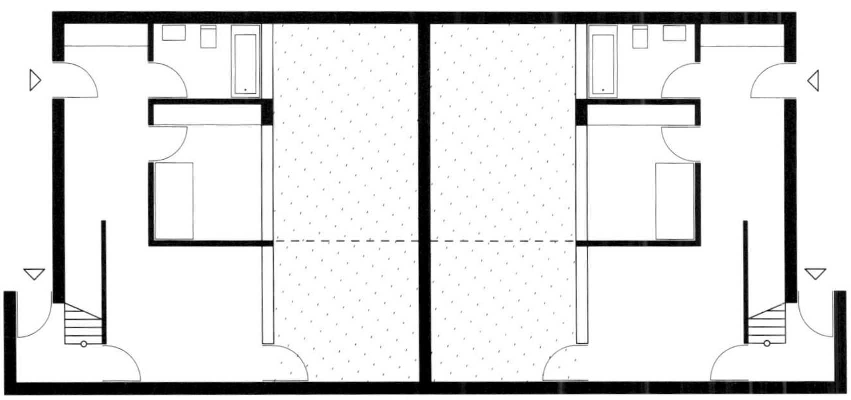

Ground floor

Student project
Darmstadt University
Duc Tuan Tong Tran

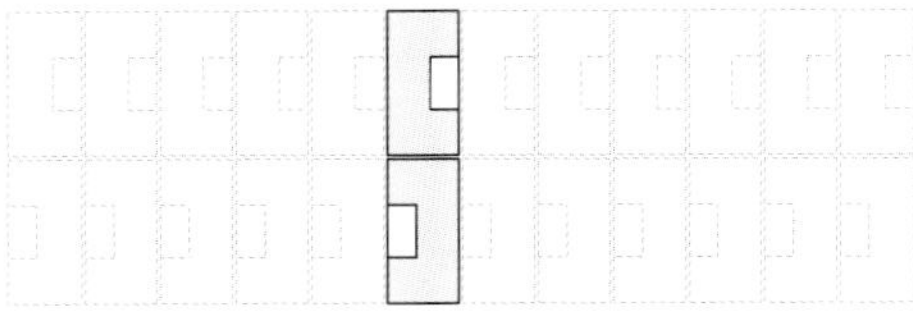

Back-to-back
Three storeys
North-south orientation

This compact back-to-back house type is characterised by the circulation zone arranged around an inner courtyard providing the house with an intimate feeling. On the ground floor, the courtyard, which serves as a transition zone between the public space and the private entrance, is accessed via a small passage. A small staircase alongside the courtyard leads up to the first floor with an open kitchen, dining area and personal room. At the front end of the building the staircase continues up to the second floor comprising also a large roof terrace. The circulation route in this small house provides an exciting path to ever-lighter spaces. Furthermore, the positioning of the hallway on the first floor alongside the party wall offers many possibilities to link to parts of adjoining units. The room facing the street could serve as a studio, office or parking space. The weak point of this type is the provision of only one bathroom located on the ground floor, which limits the house's functionality to a certain degree.

Patio houses
Amsterdam, 1998
Van Sambeek & Van Veen Architecten

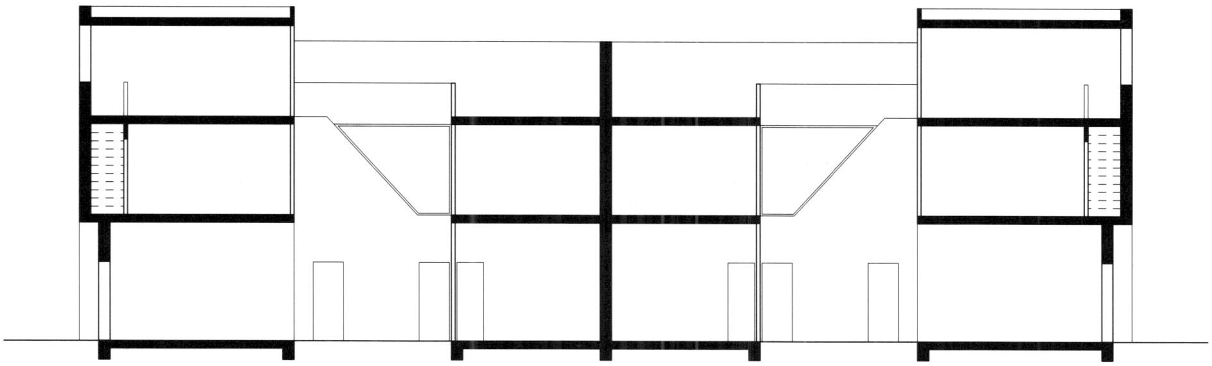

Longitudinal section

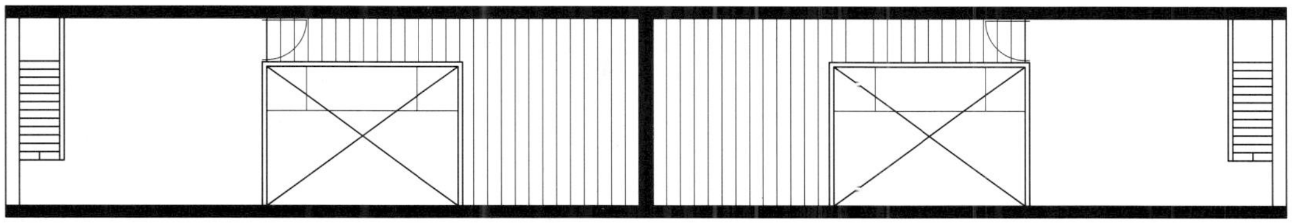

2nd upper floor

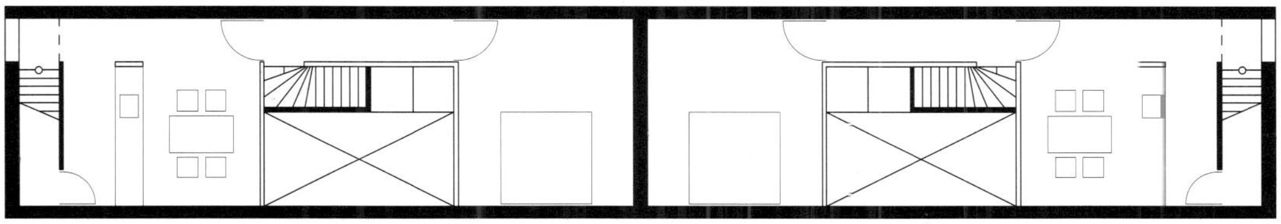

1st upper floor

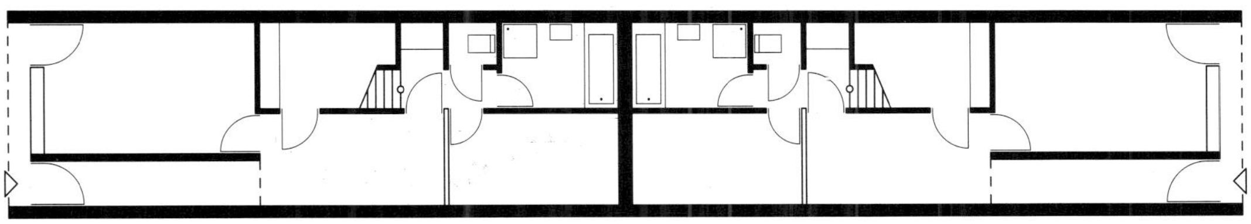

Ground floor

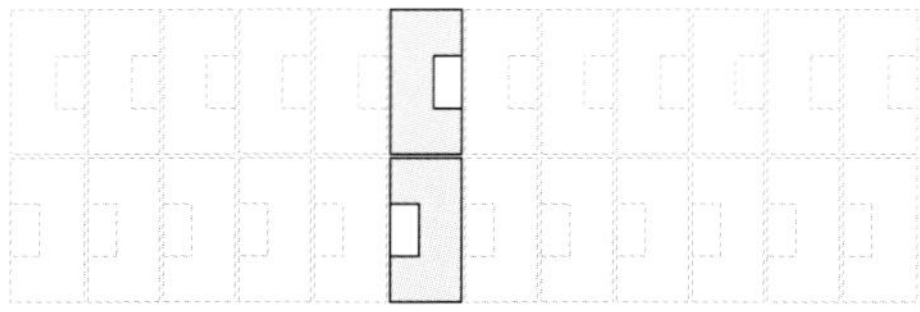

Back-to-back
Three storeys
North-south orientation

The characteristic attribute of this house type is a long, narrow living and dining room on the first floor featuring a dramatic access. The entrance to the room is located on its rear side and accessed via a spiral stair; when opening the door closing off the hallway, views through the glazed patio into the light in the living area are offered. This dramaturgy entails long circulation paths on the ground floor, which is designed as an open passage with a parking option and a small personal room. A second personal room is located on the top floor. Allocated to it is a separate bathroom receiving no daylight. The generously dimensioned roof terrace offers a secluded open space, compensating the constriction on the ground floor. The economical arrangement of building services and the organisation of the circulation space on the upper floors should be noted. The open room concept allows for a flexible use. Due to the long transition zone on the ground floor, this house type can extend right to the street frontage.

Group of houses "02 + 14"
Amsterdam, 2000
Köther & Salman

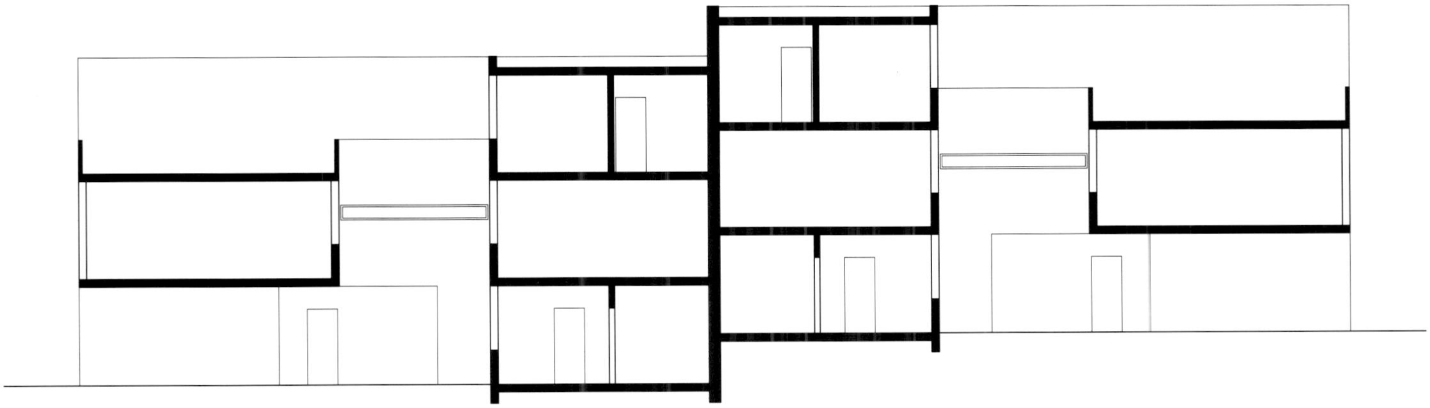

Longitudinal section

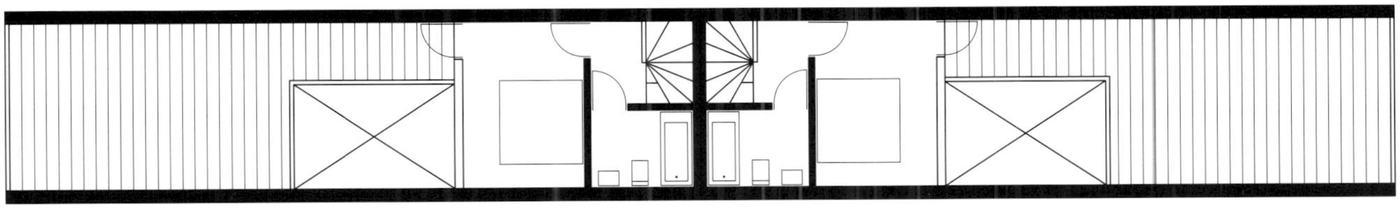

2nd upper floor

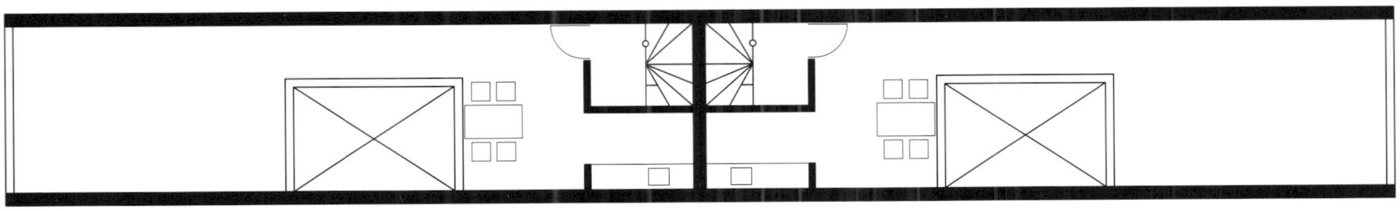

1st upper floor

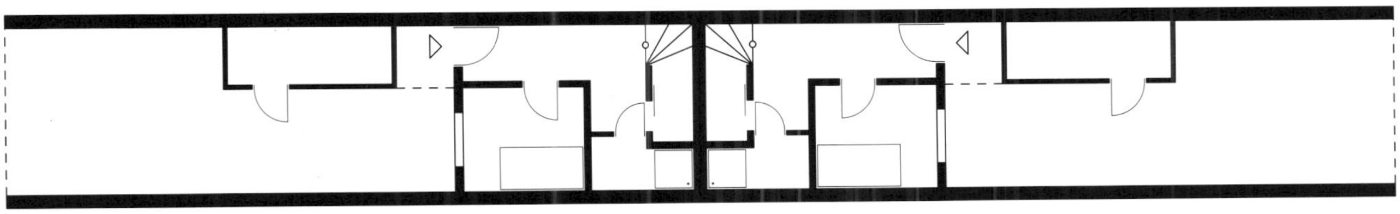

Ground floor

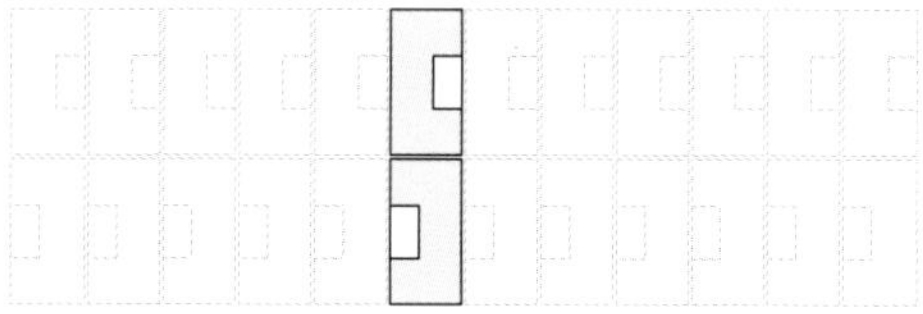

Back-to-back
Three storeys
North-south orientation

This back-to-back house type features a centrally located small inner courtyard providing daylight for the interior spaces. Since the structure covers the entire lot, extremely dense urban developments can be realised. The floor plan is divided into three zones: separate rooms in the front and back and a courtyard in the centre. Vertically, the house is also divided into three zones: the access zone on the ground floor, the high-ceiling living area on the first floor and personal rooms on the top floor. On the top floor, one personal room was traded in for an open space above the dining area. Because of the low-pitched roof, more light can reach the inner courtyard. The courtyard creates a remarkable spatial experience allowing the residents to view their own house through the window. In spite of the relatively confined space, this supports a sense of circuitousness and generous dimensions.

Group of houses
Amsterdam, 1998
Claus en Kaan Architecten

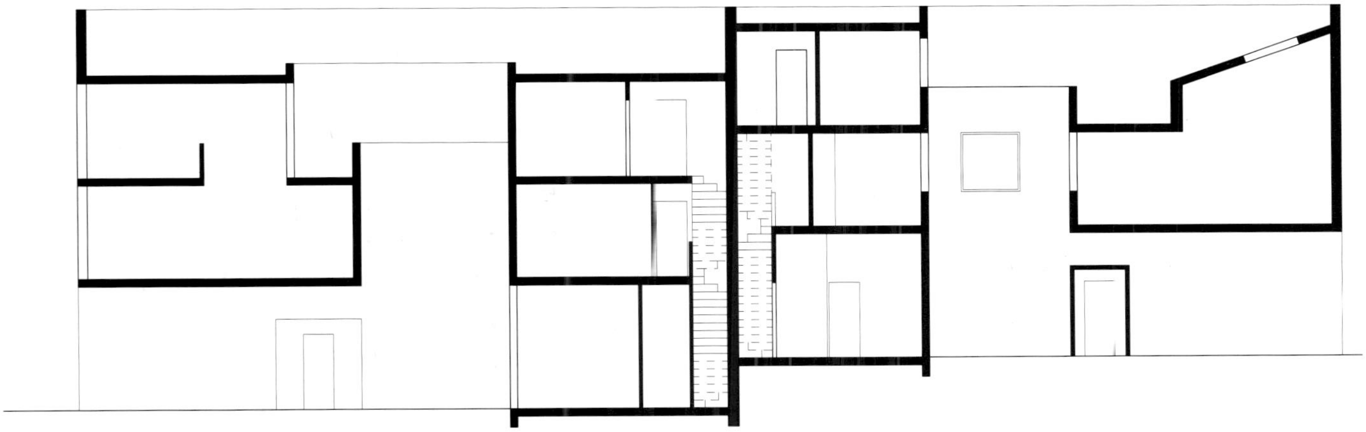

Longitudinal section

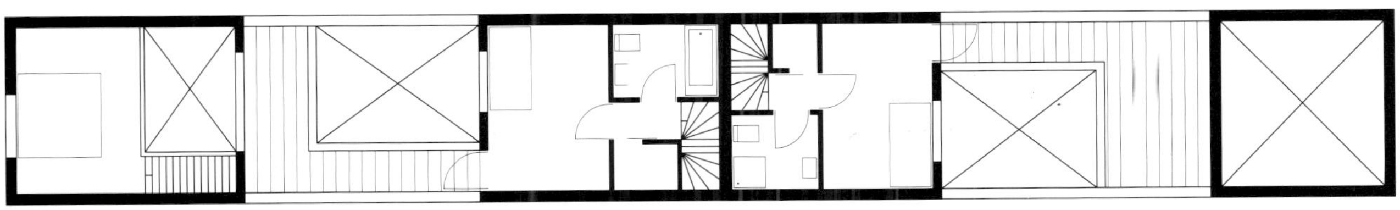

2nd upper floor

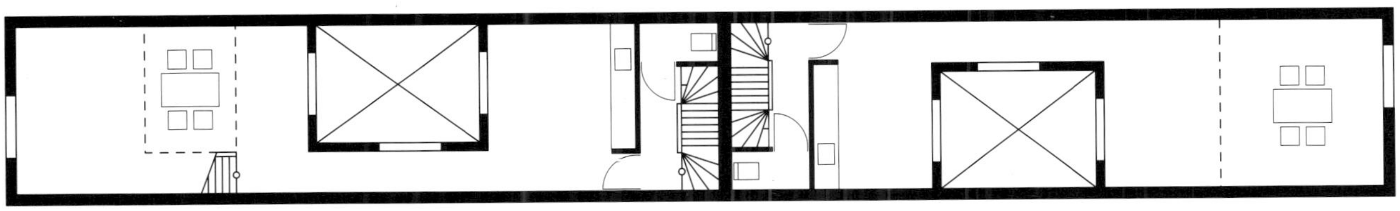

1st upper floor

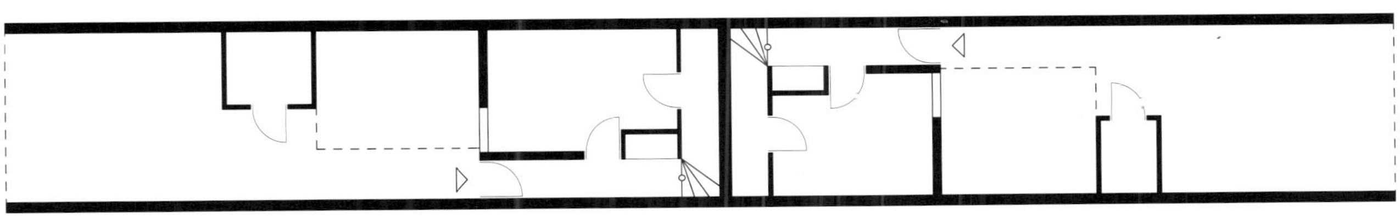

Ground floor

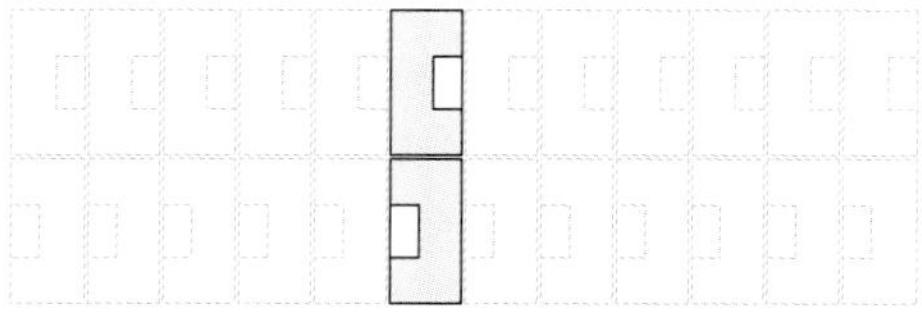

Back-to-back
Three storeys
North-south orientation

This back-to-back house type is ideal for extremely dense urban environments. It occupies little ground and neighbouring units are attached on three sides. Therefore the surface area of the house is very small in relation to its volume. The resulting energy benefits make this type a viable solution for future urban developments. Despite the density, this house type features secluded sunny open spaces in the form of roof terraces on the first and second floor. The zoning of the floor plan with the centrally positioned quarter-spiral staircase adjacent to the party wall to the neighbouring lot is actually typical for row houses. The potential for modifications of this house lies in its width and the possibility for interconnections to neighbouring units on almost all sides. Weak points of the design are the large personal room on the first floor featuring only a skylight and the bathrooms receiving no daylight.

99 patio houses
Amsterdam, 1999
Atelier Zeinstra van der Pol

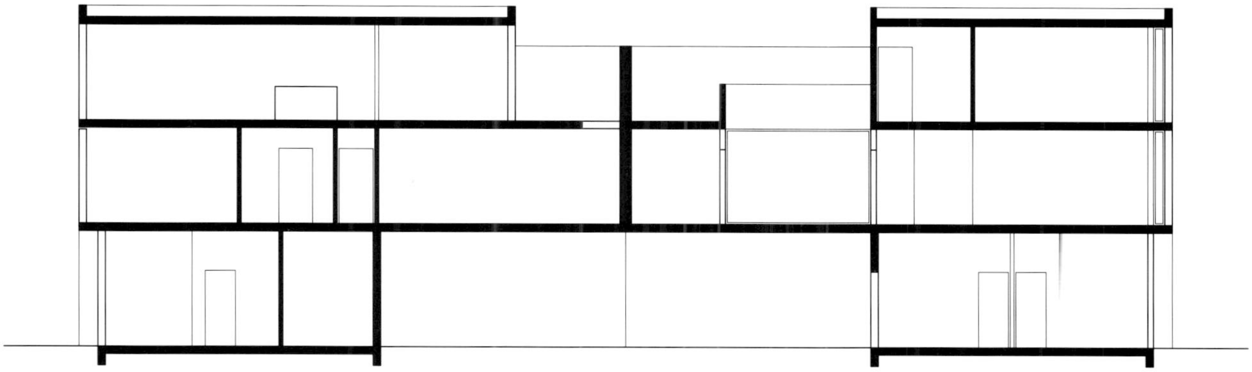

Longitudinal section

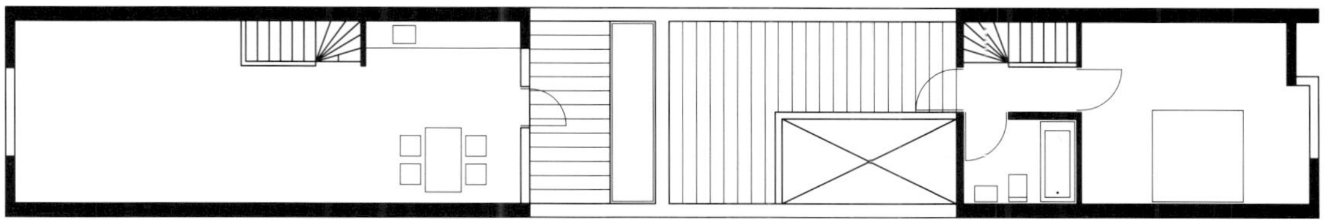

2nd upper floor

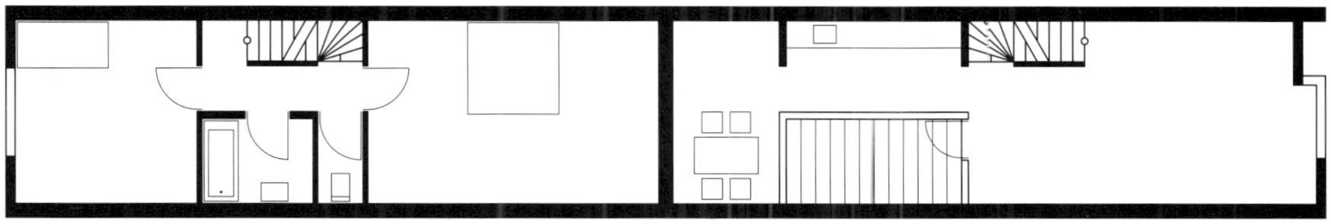

1st upper floor

Ground floor

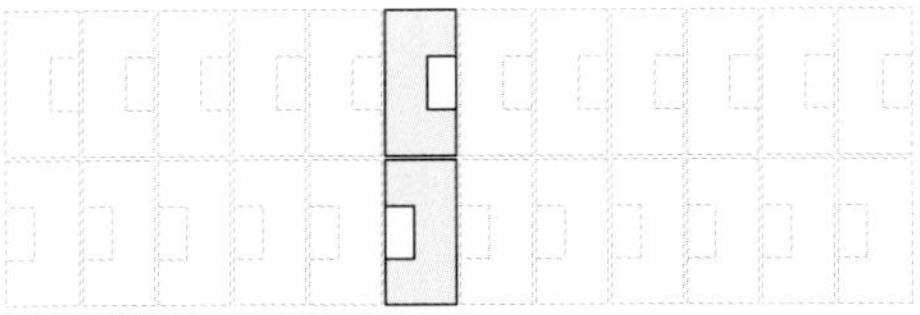

Back-to-back
Three storeys
North-south orientation

A characteristic feature of this house type is the driveway located in the centre of the ground floor. Access is gained via two entrances, one on the front side and one in the back. The width of the house – 5.50 metres – not only allows parking on the ground floor but also the arrangement of two personal rooms side by side on the top floor. The upper levels are economically accessed via a central staircase. The far end of the living area on the first floor receives daylight through an elongated skylight. Generous recesses in the building volume create secluded roof terraces and give the south-facing façade a three-dimensional character and rhythm. Large surface areas of the north façade open towards the water. As with almost all back-to-back houses, floor plans can easily be joined.

44 patio houses
Amsterdam, 1998
Kees Christiaanse architects and planners

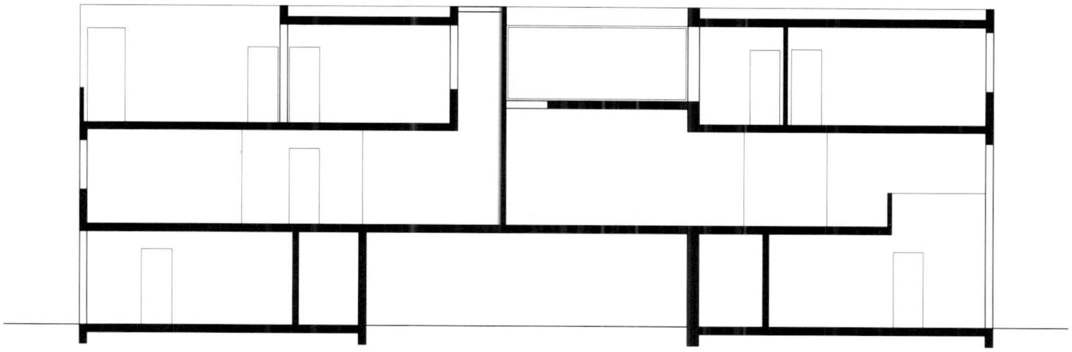

Longitudinal section

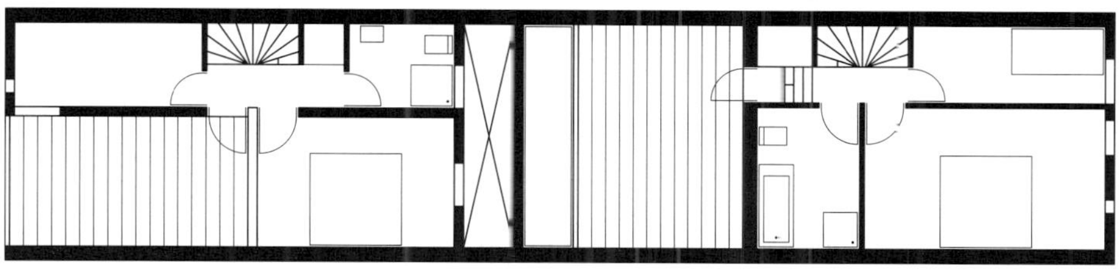

2nd upper floor

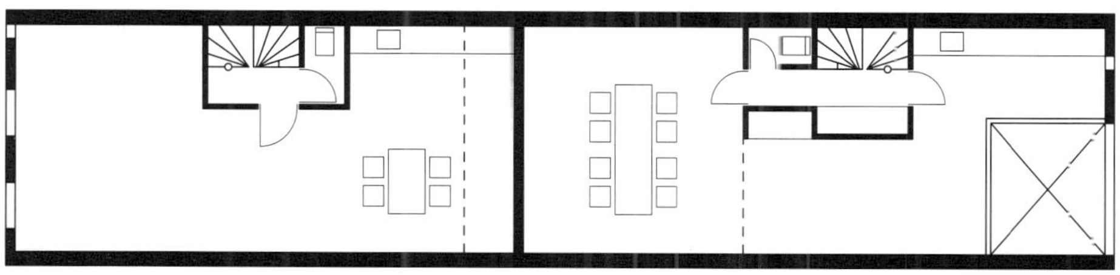

1st upper floor

Ground floor

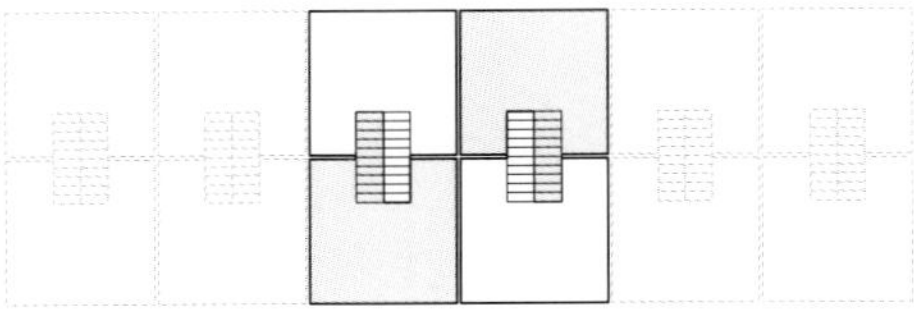

Front-to-back
Three storeys
East-west orientation

The special characteristic of this back-to-back house type are two single-flight straight staircases located at an offset in the centre of the house. Along with these staircases, the location of the flats shifts from one end of the house to the other on every level, thereby creating an interlocked spatial arrangement. This overcomes the typical one-sided orientation of back-to-back houses. In general, this type requires a secluded open space in front of the house, because most rooms are oriented towards the public space. In this example, an inner courtyard staggered across the storeys provides daylight for the centre section of the house. The first and second floors comprise large personal rooms. The courtyard offers natural light and ventilation for the bathroom. Instead of a personal room, a roof garden could be realised on the top floor. This house type can also be realised on a narrower grid, which would further enhance its cost effectiveness. However, it requires an east-west orientation.

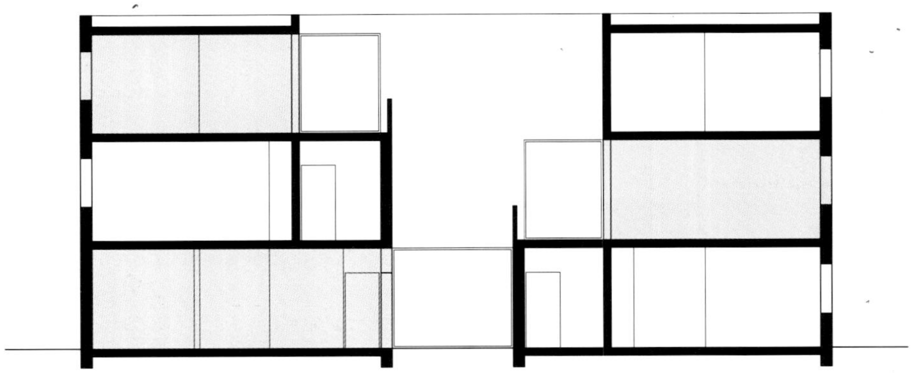

Longitudinal section

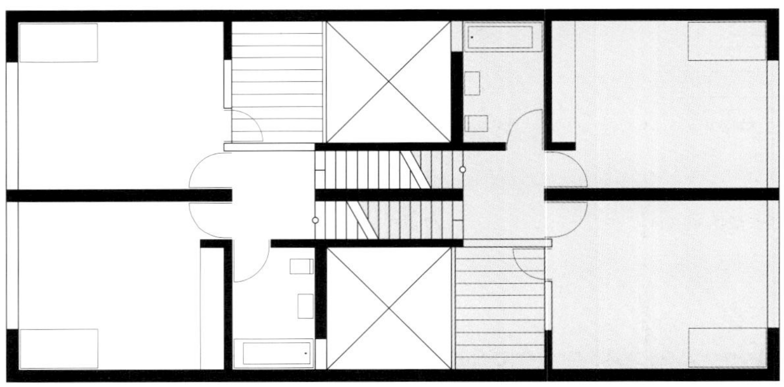

1st upper floor

Ground floor

Student project
Darmstadt University
Eva Zimmermann

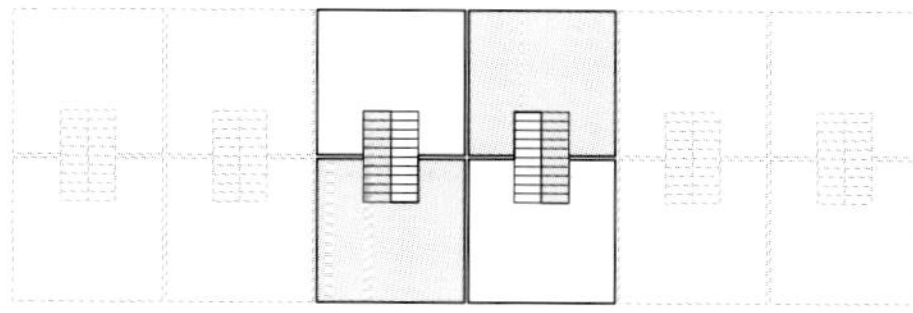

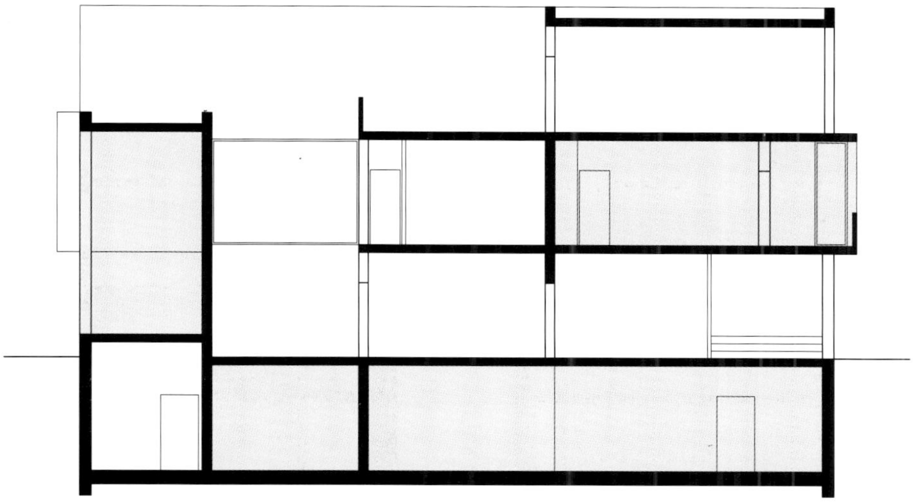

Longitudinal section

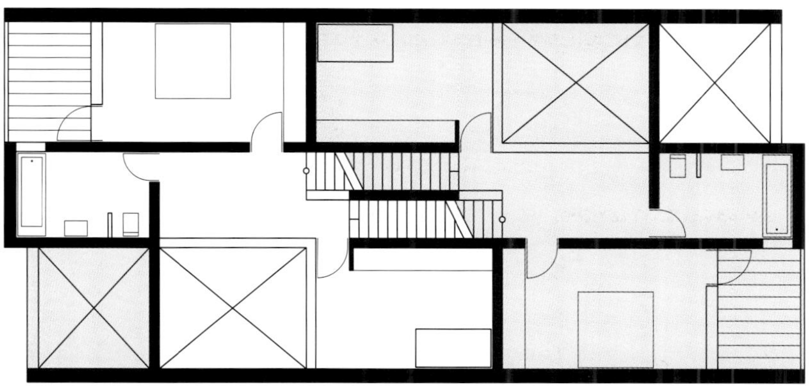

1st upper floor

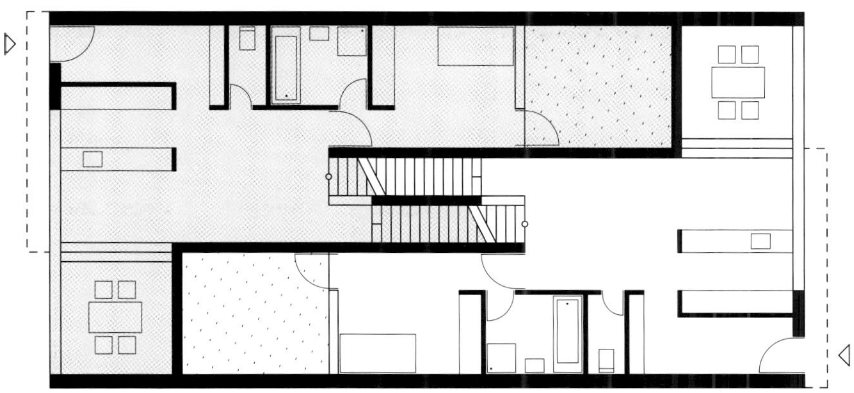

Ground floor

Front-to-back
Three storeys
East-west orientation

The apartment units are offset in section and accessed by two staircases with opposite orientation. The lengths of the units vary on the different levels. Because of the offset, each flat receives daylight from east and west. Additional courtyards provide daylight for the rear area of the longer section of each unit featuring a personal room and a bathroom on the ground floor. The dining area is slightly raised above the living area. A generously dimensioned porch – protected by the shift of the façade on the first floor – constitutes the transition zone between public space and the flats. The personal rooms on the first floor are accessed via a workspace mezzanine adjacent to the courtyard. On the second floor, two additional personal rooms and a roof terrace are located. Hardly any mono-functional hallways are to be found in the house. Due to the interlocking arrangement of the two types, structural solutions to soundproof the individual units need to be worked out. This complex house type allows very little modification or expansion.

Darmstadt University
Student project
Claudia Wall

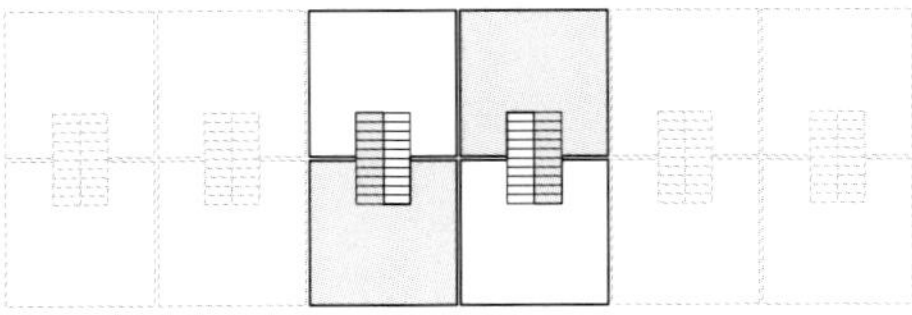

Front-to-back
Three storeys
East-west orientation

In this back-to-back house type the orientation changes on every level. The apartment units are interlocked with each other so that the side that is exposed to daylight changes while ascending or descending the single-flight staircase. This not only ensures multiple daylight conditions but also makes for varied visual connections to the urban surroundings. Open spaces in the form of courtyards, terraces and loggias create diverse relationships to the exterior. On the ground floor, an entry zone offering storage space separates the street space from an intimate courtyard in front of the bedroom and from a terrace courtyard in front of the dining area. On the first floor, a living room, loggia, toilet and storage are situated at the other end of the house. On the second floor, there are two additional personal rooms with adjoining loggias, separated from each other by a bathroom with shower and a separate toilet. Due to the centrally located entrance and the inner staircase, the potential for modifications of this house type is rather low.

Student project
Darmstadt University
Christoph Winterling

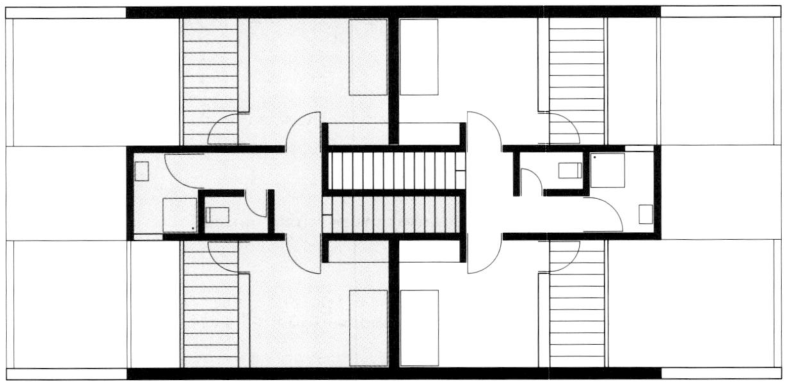

2nd upper floor

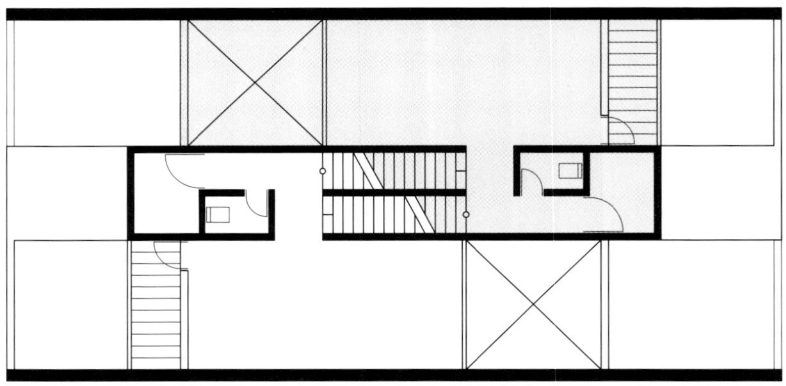

1st upper floor

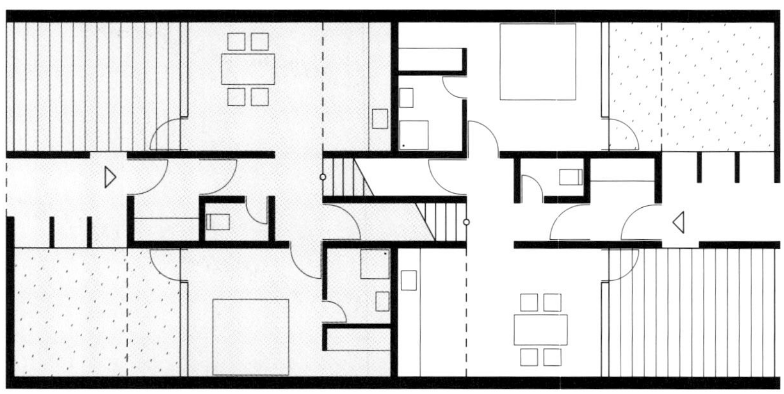

Ground floor

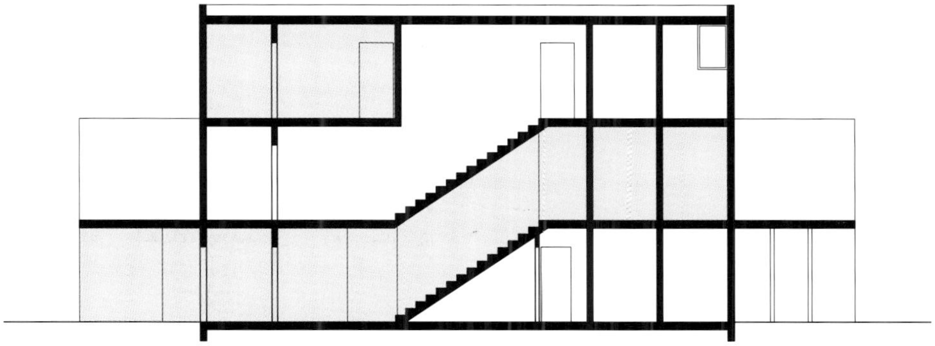

Longitudinal section

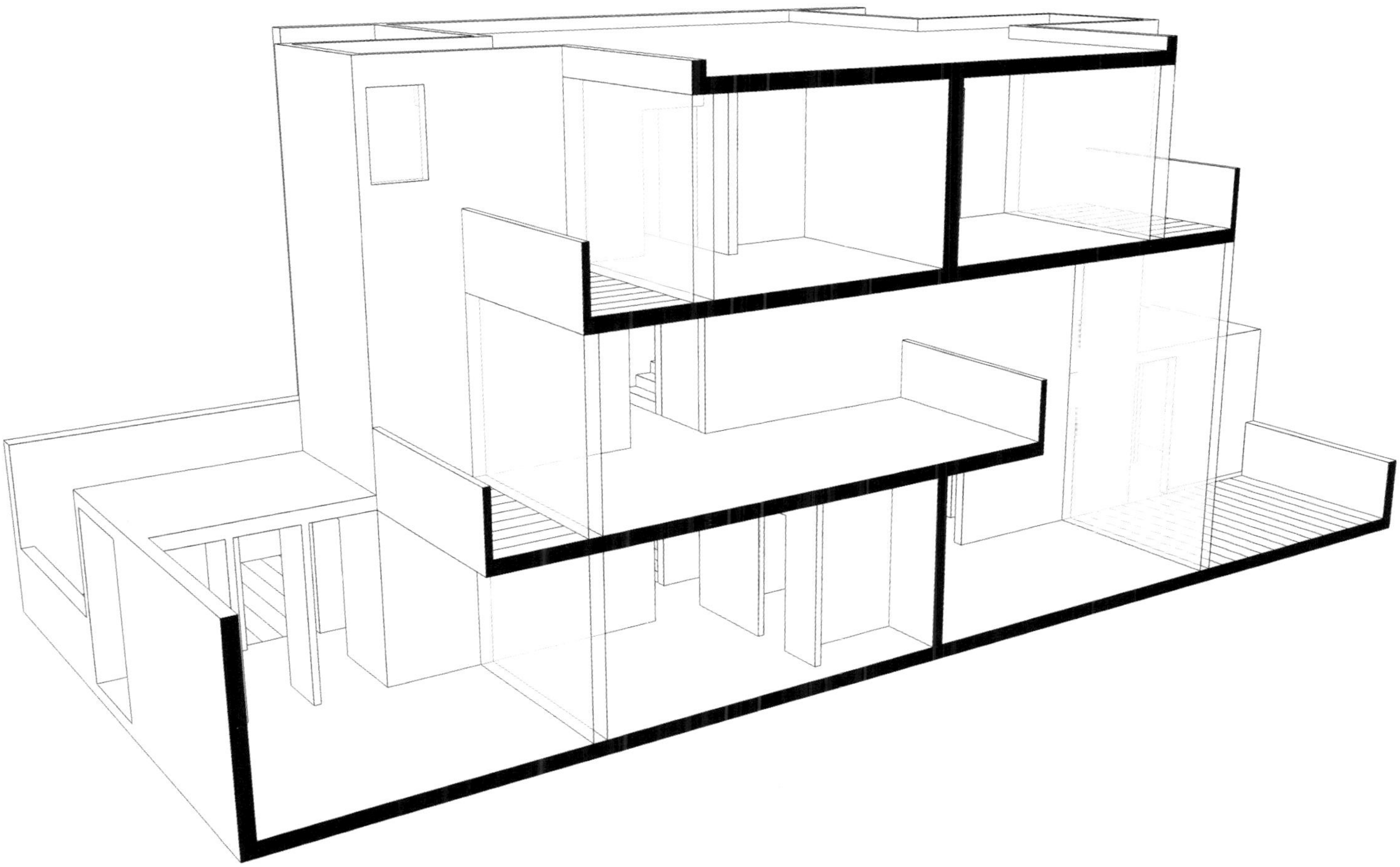

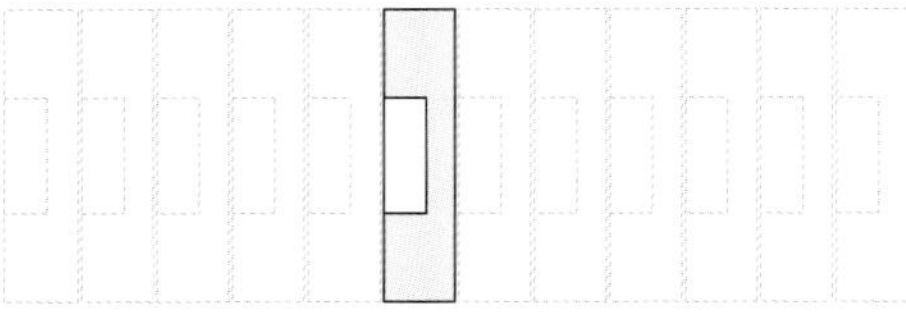

Back-to-back, "vis-à-vis"
Five storeys
East-west orientation

Only the lower levels of this house type are attached to the neighbouring unit. Two independent residential towers extend above the first floor. Thus, the complex could combine commercially used spaces on the lower levels with separate residential units on the upper floors. The arrangement of the commercial units is flexible, which represents a structural advantage. However, this type does not offer a solution to prevent views from one unit into the other. The two dwellings share a common terrace and the inescapable visual contact between the units calls for close contact between the two parties. Here, typical boundaries between neighbouring units are broken up in favour of an open structure. The straight staircases with their lower and upper landings in the two towers allow for linking adjoining units on all levels. In practice, the extreme layout with only one room per level might prove problematic.

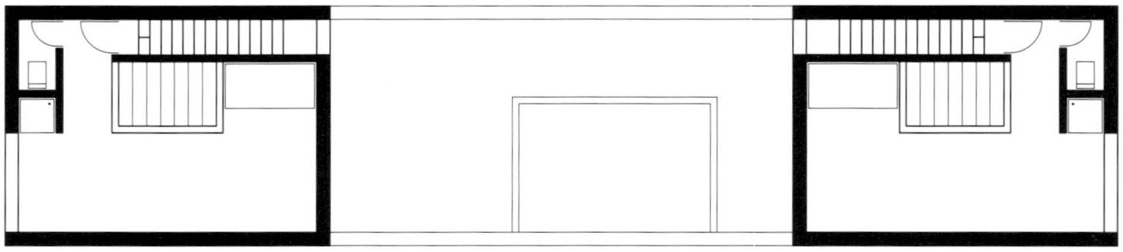

4th upper floor

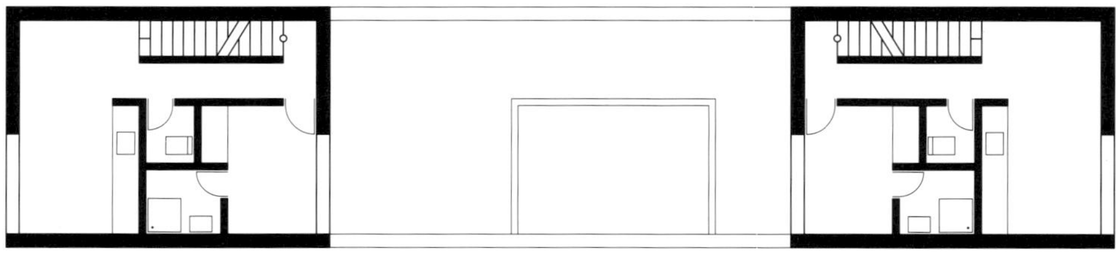

3rd upper floor

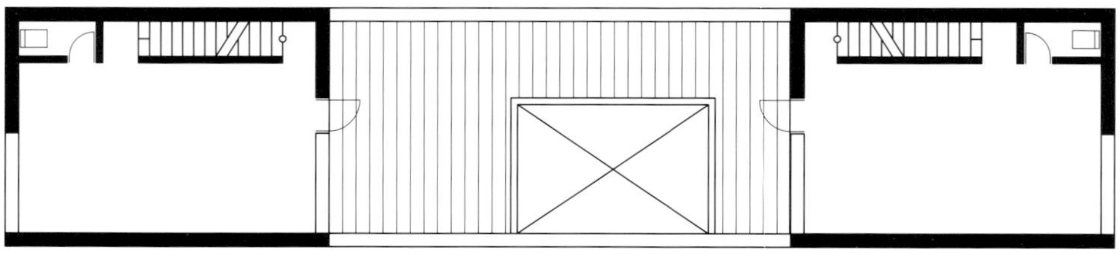

2nd upper floor

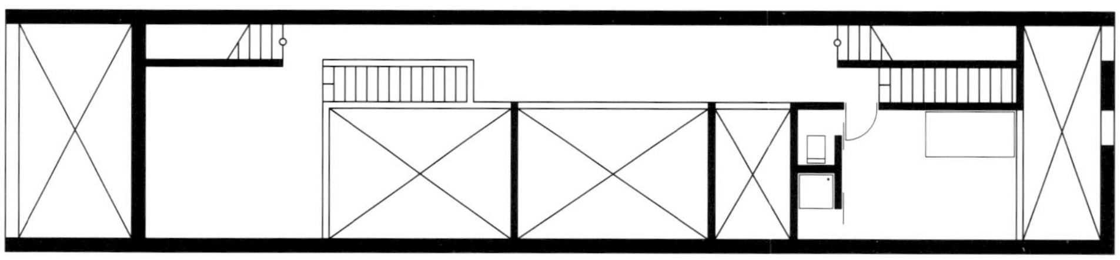

1st upper floor

Student project
Darmstadt University
Gabriele Pinter

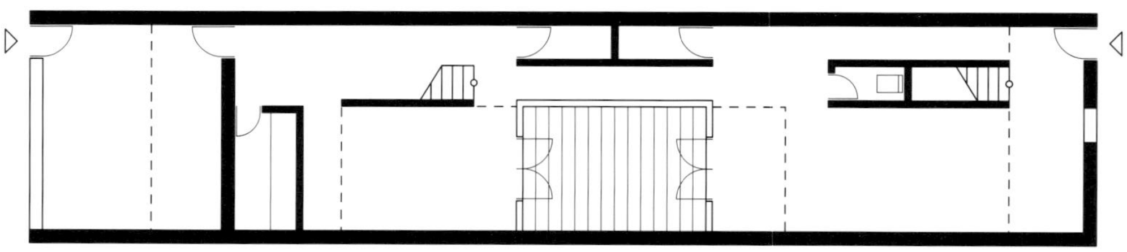

Ground floor

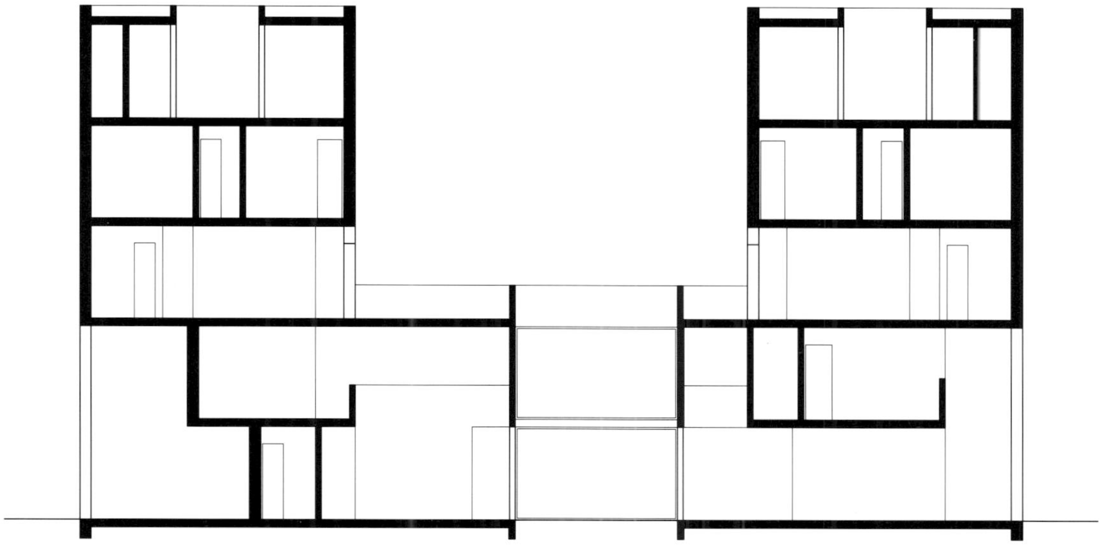

Longitudinal section

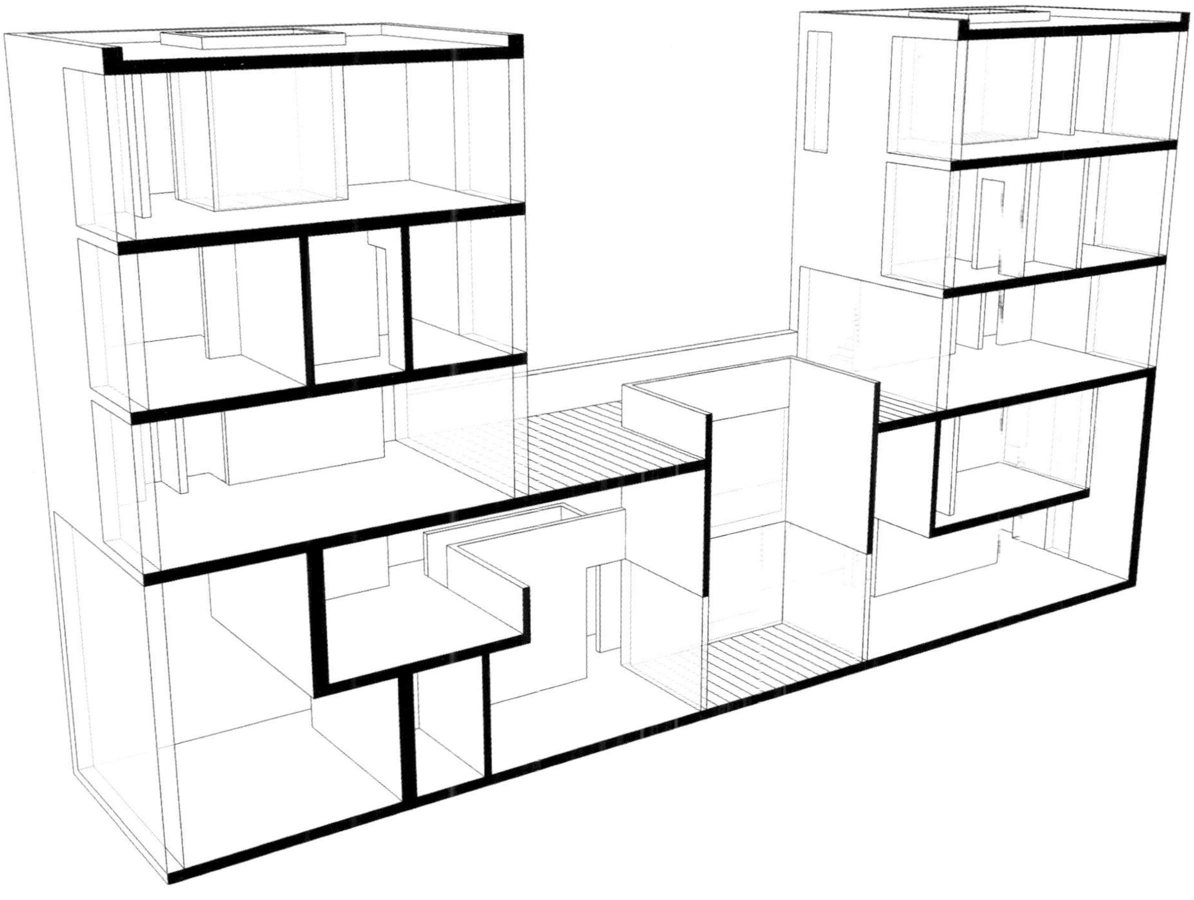

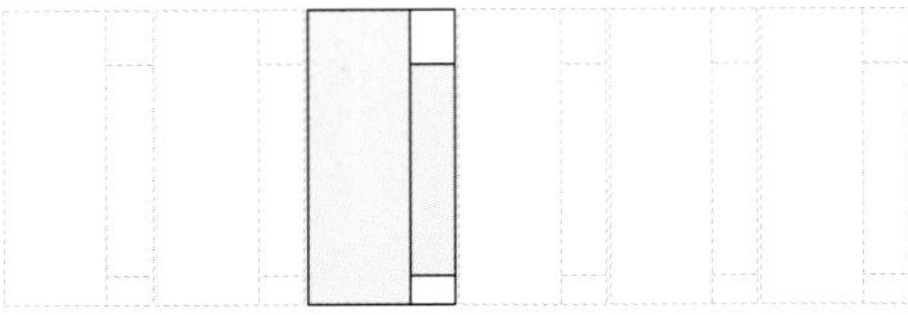

Two-zone house
Single storey
North-south orientation

The floor plan of this house type is divided into two zones with different room temperatures to reduce energy consumption. Besides this measure of passive energy conservation, another element is used to enable active energy gains. In the centre of the "warm" living area a two-storey glasshouse extends beyond the roof. As a consequence, kitchen, dining area and living room are grouped around this energy source. Adjacent to this zone, personal rooms requiring lower temperatures are to be found. These in turn are grouped around the bathrooms, which again should have a higher room temperature. Thus, the typology of the floor plan is derived from energy aspects. As half of the flat structure is buried in the ground, the house sits inconspicuously in the landscape. This also minimises the building's surface area exposed to the elements. A roof garden open to all sides and secluded inner courtyards create generously dimensioned exterior spaces of varying atmospheres.

Group of houses
Berlin, 1985
Herzog + Partner

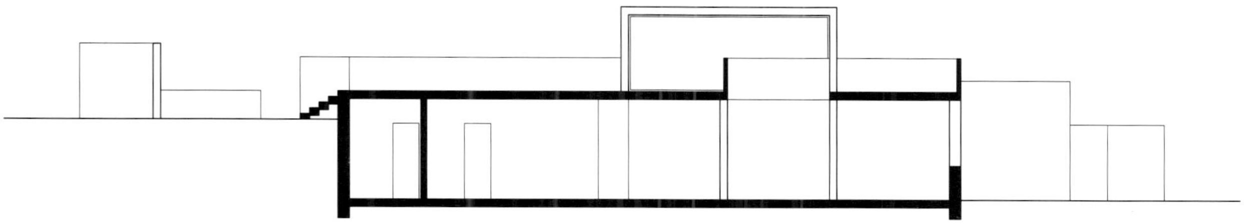

Longitudinal section

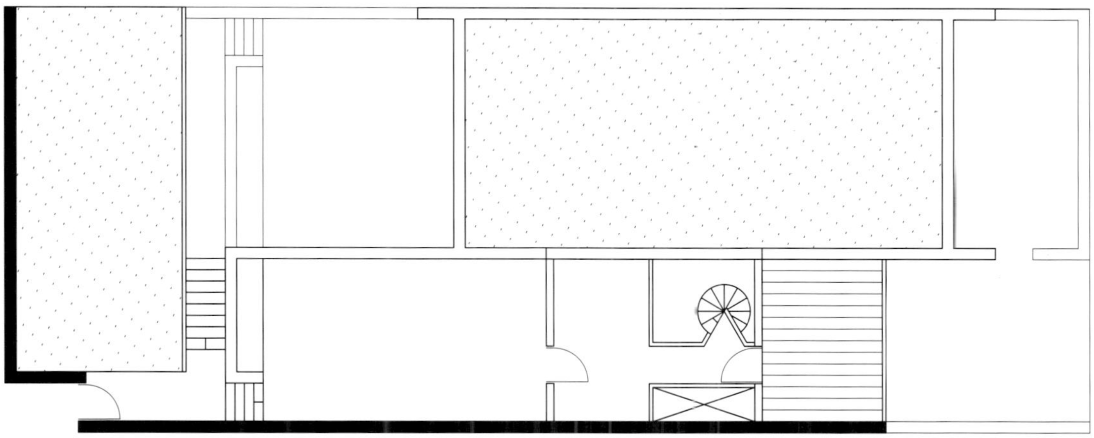

Upper floor

Ground floor

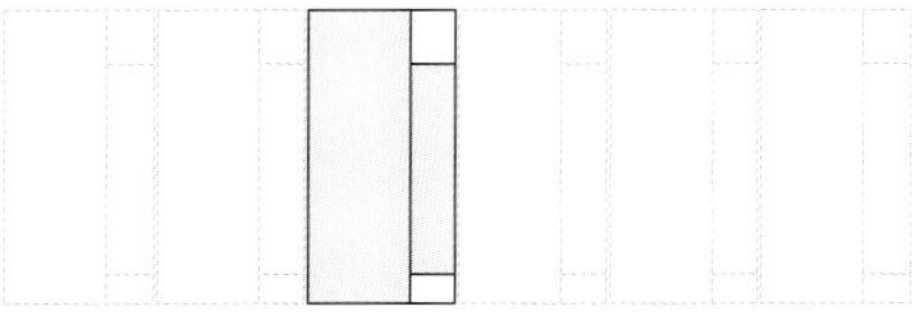

Two-zone house
Two storeys
East-west orientation

The floor plan of this house type is divided into a two-storey "warm" living room zone and a one-storey "cold" zone with secondary rooms. In this design, personal rooms are defined as "warm" rooms and bathrooms as "cold" rooms. While the zoning of the floor plan in this example is not as consistently derived from energy demands (as is the previous example), this house type provides more flexibility in terms of usage. Identically shaped personal rooms are grouped around a central double-height space with a hallway wrapped around it. The principal organisation of the internal circulation enables linking this house type to adjoining units on every level. The possibility of externally accessing the upper level via the roof of the secondary room zone opens up additional possibilities for flexible uses. The double-height space could be developed into an "energy garden" with a glass roof to realise heat gains.

Group of houses "Kranichstein"
Darmstadt, 1983
Herzog + Partner

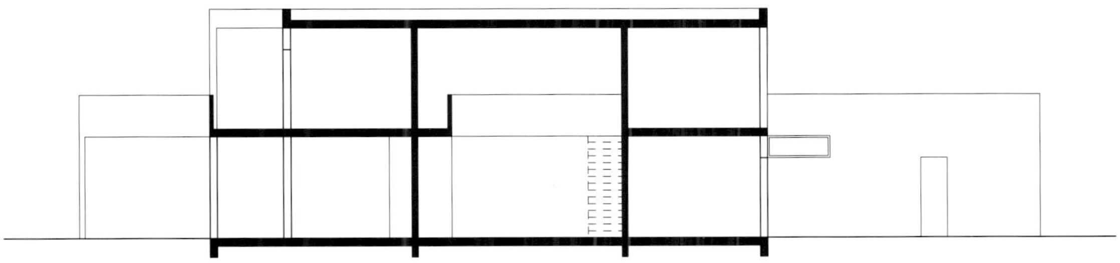

Longitudinal section

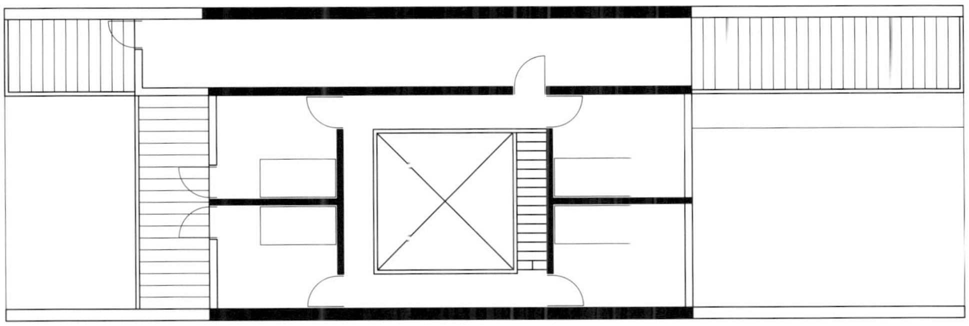

Upper floor

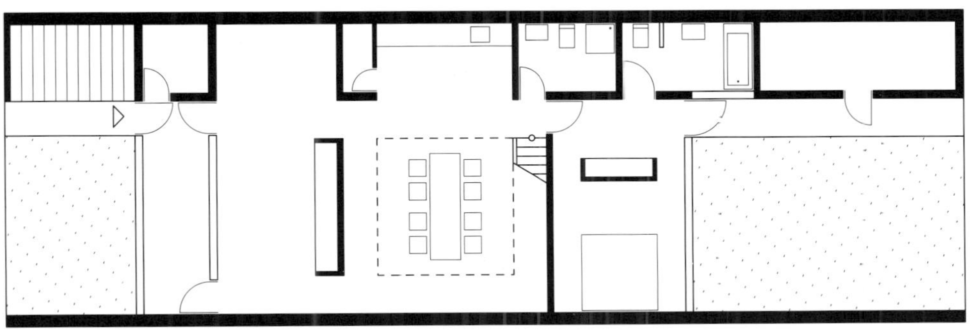

Ground floor

Bibliography

Alder, Michael; Althaus, Peter F.; Giovanoli, Diego (Ed.): *Palazzine in Soazza .Die Typologie des Korridorhauses/Palazzine a Soazza. La tipologia della casa a corridoio*. Basel, Boston, Berlin: Birkhäuser 1995

Argan, Giulio Carlo: "On the Typology of Architecture", in: *Architectural Design*, no. 12, 1963, p. 561-562

Brenner, Klaus Theo; Geisert, Helmut: *Das städtische Reihenhaus. Geschichte und Typologie*. Stuttgart: Karl Krämer 2004

Caminada, Gion: *Stiva da Morts. Vom Nutzen der Architektur*. Zurich: gta-Verlag 2003

Caminada, Gion: *Cul zuffel e l'aura dado*. Lucerne: Quart Verlag 2005

Faller, Peter: *Der Wohngrundriss*. Wüstenrot foundation, Munich: DVA 2002

Flagge, Ingeborg (Ed.): *Geschichte des Wohnens*. Vol. 1-5., 2nd edition; Wüstenrot foundation, Munich: DVA 1999

Frampton, Kenneth: *Atelier 5. Siedlungen und städtebauliche Projekte*. Wiesbaden: Vieweg 1994

Harlander, Tilman: *Villa und Eigenheim: Suburbaner Städtebau in Deutschland*. Wüstenrot foundation, Munich: DVA 2001

Heider, Katharina: *Doppelhäuser und Reihenhäuser. Aktuelle Beispiele zeitgenössischer Architektur*. Munich: DVA 2006

Kottje, Johannes: *Reihenhäuser Doppelhäuser. Mit Architekten kostengünstig und hochwertig bauen*. Munich: DVA 2004

Krier, Rob: *Architecture and Urban Design*, London: Academy Editions 1993

Krier, Léon: *Houses, Palaces, Cities*, London: Academy Editions 1995

Krier, Rob; Graves, Michael; Ibelings, Hans; Meuser, Philipp; Bodenschatz, Harald: *Town Spaces*, 2nd revised edition; Basel, Berlin, Boston: Birkhäuser 2006

Lack, Peter: *Bruno Reichlins gebaute Architekturkritik*, VDG Verlag and the databank for human sciences, 2nd edition; Weimar 1995, p. 93/94

Maretto, Paolo: *La casa veneziana nella storia della citta, dalle origini all' Ottocen-*

to. 4th edition; Venice: Marsilio Editori 1992

Mehlhorn, Dieter-Jürgen; Tiedemann, Marita: *Grundrissatlas Wohnungsbau Spezial. Lösungen und Projektbeispiele für: Schwierige Grundstücke, Besondere Lagen. Erweiterung, Umnutzung, Aufstockung*. Berlin: Bauwerk 2000

Moneo, Rafael: "On Typology", in: *Oppositions*, 1978, no 13, p. 23-45

Quincy, Quatremère de: *Encyclopédie méthodique d'Architecture*, Paris 1825

Rogers, Ernesto: "The problem of building within an existing environment", in: *Zodiac*, no. 3, 1990, p. 8-11

Rossi, Aldo: *The Architecture of the City*. Cambridge: MIT Press 1982

Rossi, Aldo: *Das Konzept des Typus*, in: Arch+, no. 37, 1978, p. 39 ff.

Schittich, Christian (Ed.): In Detail: *High-Density Housing: Concepts, Planning Construction*. Basel, Boston, Berlin: Birkhäuser 2004

Schittich, Christian (Ed.): In Detail. *Single Family Houses*. New enlarged edition; Basel, Boston, Berlin: Birkhäuser 2005

Schneider, Friederike (Ed.): *Floor Plan Manual Housing*. 3rd revised and expanded edition; Basel, Boston, Berlin: Birkhäuser 2004

Schramm, Helmut: *Low Rise – High Density: Horizontale Verdichtungsformen im Wohnbau*. Vienna: Springer 2005

Teut, Anna: "Von Typen und Normen, Maßreglern und Maßregelungen", in: *Architektur und technisches Denken*, Daidalos no.18, Dec. 15th 1985, p. 53

Waechter-Böhm, Liesbeth (Ed.): *House-ing. Carlo Baumschlager & Dietmar Eberle*. Vienna, New York: Springer 2000

Zophoniasson-Baierl, Ulrike (Ed.): *Michael Alder. Das Haus als Typ*. Basel, Boston, Berlin: Birkhäuser 2006

Illustration credits

Ignacio Martinez
25
Sebastian Schaal | Martin Trefon
27, 31, 34, 41, 44, 53, 55, 57, 90, 92
94, 96, 98
Walter Stamm-Teske
28
Francesca Giovanelli
33, 65
Günter R. Wett
43
d-company
46
schneider+schumacher
48
Rolf Mühlethaler
59
AV 1
61
Piet Rook
63
Eduard Hueber
67
Herman Hertzberger
73
Oscar Gil Delgado
80
Michael Heinrich
83
Ottokar Uhl
106
Verena Herzog-Loibl
108